Contents

Published by HarperCollins*Publishers* Limited
77–85 Fulham Palace Road
Hammersmith
London
W6 8JB

Browse the complete Collins catalogue at
www.collinseducation.com

10 9 8 7

ISBN-13 978-0-00-713872-2
ISBN-10 0-00-713872-5

British Library Cataloguing in Publication Data
A Catalogue record for this publication is available from the British Library

Edited by First Class Publishing
Project Management by Sam Holmes
Covers by Tim Byrne
Designed and illustrated by Barking Dog Art
Production by Emma Johnson
Printed and bound by Martins the Printers Ltd, Berwick upon Tweed

The publishers would like to thank the many teachers and advisers whose
feedback helped to shape *Maths Frameworking*.

Every effort has been made to trace copyright holders and to obtain their permission
for the use of copyright material. The author and publishers will gladly receive
any information enabling them to rectify any error or omission in subsequent editions.

You might also like to visit:
www.harpercollins.co.uk
The book lover's website

Mixed Sources
Product group from well-managed
forests and other controlled sources
www.fsc.org Cert no. SW-COC-1806
© 1996 Forest Stewardship Council
FSC

Practice

1A Negative numbers

1 Calculate these.

   a $5 - 9$ **b** $2 - 6 + 3$ **c** $-2 + -5$ **d** $9 - -7$ **e** $-3 - +5 - 4$

2 **i** Add each number to the number on its left. Write down your answers.
   ii Subtract each number from the number on its left. Write down your answers.

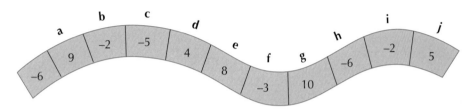

3 Calculate these.

   a 5×-3 **b** -8×-5 **c** -3×10 **d** -2×-2
   e 14×-3 **f** $-4 \times -2 \times 5$ **g** $2 \times -3 \times -1$ **h** $-10 \times 6 \times -10$
   i $16 \div -2$ **j** $-6 \div -6$ **k** $-9 \div 3$ **l** $12 \div -3$
   m $-100 \div 10$ **n** $20 \div -2 \div -5$ **o** $-36 \div -3 \div -4$ **p** $40 \div -5 \div -2$

4 Copy and complete these chains of calculations.

   a

   b

   c

5 **a** Write down five calculations involving $\times$ that give the answer -6.
   b Write down five calculations involving $\div$ that give the answer -5.

6 Calculate these.

   a $(-8)^2$ **b** $4 + -2 \times 7$ **c** $-14 \div 2 + 5$
   d $2 \times -6 \div -3$ **e** $4 \times (-3 - 5)$ **f** $-8 - (7 + 5)$
   g $(-3 - 12) \div -3$

7 Put brackets in to make each of these calculations true.

a $9 \times -2 + 1 = -9$ **b** $-4 + -6 \div -2 = -1$ **c** $5 - 7 + 2 - 4 = -8$

8 **a** $20 \div (-2)^2$ **b** $(-5 - 3)^2$ **c** $5 + 4 \times (-3)^2$ **d** $40 - (4 - 9)^2$

Practice

1B HCF and LCM

1 **a** Write the first 10 multiples of these numbers.
    i 3   **ii** 6   **iii** 8   **iv** 15
    b Use your answers to **a** to find the LCM of each of these pairs of numbers.
    i 3 and 8   **ii** 6 and 15   **iii** 6 and 8   **iv** 8 and 15

2 **a** Write out all the factors of these numbers.
    i 12   **ii** 18   **iii** 20   **iv** 30
    b Use your answers to **a** to find the HCF of each of these pairs of numbers.
    i 12 and 18   **ii** 12 and 20   **iii** 20 and 30   **iv** 18 and 20

3 Find the LCM.

    a 4 and 8   **b** 6 and 10   **c** 7 and 8   **d** 9 and 12

4 Find the HCF.

    a 14 and 35   **b** 8 and 20   **c** 12 and 30   **d** 15 and 24

5 **a** Two numbers have a LCM of 20 and a HCF of 2. What are they?
    b Two numbers have a LCM of 36 and a HCF of 6. What are they?
    c Two numbers have a LCM of 30 and a HCF of 1. What could they be?

6 The LCM of two numbers is twice their HCF. What can you say about the two numbers? Investigate.

Practice

1C Powers and roots

1 Find the cubes of these numbers. Do *not* use your calculator.

    a 5   **b** 11   **c** 12

2 Calculate these powers. Do *not* use your calculator.

    a 6^4 **b** $(-2)^3$ **c** $(-4)^4$ **d** $(-10)^5$

3 Use your calculator to find these.

    a 24^2 **b** 15^3 **c** 25^3
    d 6.6^2 **e** 4.2^3 **f** 7.3^3

4 Find four cube numbers that are also multiples of 3.

5 Use your calculator to find these.

    a 2^6 **b** 4^5 **c** 8^4 **d** 6^6 **e** 3^8

6 Write down the values of these roots.

  a $\sqrt{16}$ **b** $\sqrt{81}$ **c** $\sqrt[3]{64}$ **d** $\sqrt[3]{343}$

7 For each equation, find two values of x that make the equation true.

  a $x^2 = 49$ **b** $x^2 = 100$ **c** $x^2 = 225$ **d** $x^2 = 1.44$

8 **a** Use your calculator to find these.
     i 0.4^2 **ii** 0.5^2
  b What do you think will be the answer to 0.6^2? Try it and see.
  c What do you think will be the answer to 0.3^2? Try it and see.
  d Copy and complete this table.

Number	0.1	0.2	0.3	0.4	0.5	0.6	0.7	0.8	0.9	1
Square										

9 **a** Choose any number between 0 and 1, e.g. 0.4.
  b Calculate increasing powers of your number, e.g. 0.4^2, 0.4^3, 0.4^4, etc.
  c What do you notice about the sizes of your answers as the power increases? Explain why this happens.

10 **a** Find two square numbers that have exactly one cube number between them. Write all three numbers down in order.
  b Find two cube numbers that have exactly two square numbers between them. Write all four numbers down in order.

11 **a** Use your calculator to find these.
     i 0.5^3 **ii** 0.6^3

  Look at your table of cubes.
  b What do you think will be the answer to 0.7^3? Try it and see.
  c What do you think will be the answer to 0.4^3? Try it and see.
  d What do you think will be the answer to 0.2^3? Try it and see.
  e Copy and complete this table.

Number	0.1	0.2	0.3	0.4	0.5	0.6	0.7	0.8	0.9	1
Cube										

Practice

1D Prime factors

1 Calculate these products of prime factors.

  a $2 \times 5 \times 5$ **b** $2^3 \times 3$ **c** $2 \times 3 \times 7^2$

2 Use a prime factor tree to write each of these numbers as a product of its prime factors.

  a 6   **b** 18   **c** 32   **d** 70   **e** 36

3 Use the division method to write each of these numbers as a product of its prime factors.

    a 14   **b** 45   **c** 96   **d** 130   **e** 200

4 Calculate the HCF and LCM of each pair of numbers. Use the diagrams to help.

a   **b**   **c**

5 $40 = 2 \times 2 \times 2 \times 5$ and $84 = 2 \times 2 \times 3 \times 7$

Make a diagram as in Question 4. Use the diagram to find the HCF and LCM of 40 and 84.

6 Use prime factors to calculate the HCF and LCM of each of these pairs of numbers.

    a 60 and 135   **b** 48 and 80   **c** 70 and 126

1E Sequences 1

1 Follow these instructions to generate sequences.

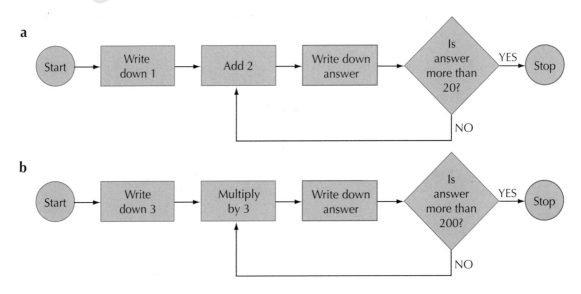

2 Draw a flow diagram to generate the sequence that starts with 10 and uses the term-to-term rule 'add 5'.

3 **a** Describe how these sequences are generated.
    i 5, 8, 11, 14, 17 …   **ii** 2, 10, 50, 250 …
   b Find the next two numbers in each sequence.

4 You are given a start number and a multiplier. Write down the first five terms of the sequence.

    a Start 1, multiplier 20   **b** Start 64, multiplier $\frac{1}{4}$
    c Start −3, multiplier −2

5 These patterns of dots generate sequences of numbers.

    a

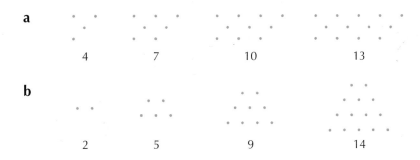

         4   7   10   13

    b

         2   5   9   14

    i Draw the next two patterns of dots.
    ii Write down the next four numbers in the sequence.

1F Sequences 2

1 For each of these arithmetic sequences, write down the first term *a* and the constant difference *d*.

    a 6, 8, 10, 12, 14, …   **b** 30, 35, 40, 45, …   **c** 100, 96, 92, 88, …

2 Given first term *a* and the constant difference *d*, write down the first six terms of each sequence.

    a $a = 7, d = 6$ **b** $a = 2, d = 2.5$ **c** $a = 8, d = −5$

3 This diagram can be used to generate sequences.

Write down the sequences generated using these values of *A* and *L*.

	A	**Term-to-term rule**	*L*
a	2	Treble	100
b	20	Subtract 3	−10
c	1	Add 2, 4, 6, 8 etc.	30
d	1	Multiply by 4, subtract 10	−600
e	500	Divide by 10	0.001

4 Write down a first term *A* and a term-to-term rule that you can use in the flow diagram in Question 3 so that

   a each term of the sequence is a negative odd number
   b the first three terms are positive, and the remainder are negative
   c the first three terms are whole numbers, and the remainder are decimal fractions.

5 **i** The *n*th term of each sequence is given below. Write down the first five terms.
   ii What is the constant difference in each sequence?

   a $3n - 1$ **b** $2n + 5$ **c** $5n - 3$ **d** $10n + 10$

Practice

1G Solving problems

1 Paving slabs 1 metre square are used for borders around L-shaped ponds.

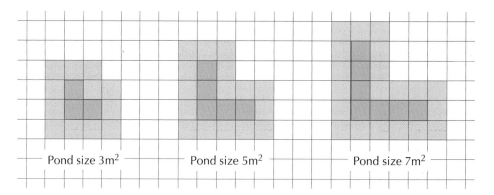

   Pond size 3m²   Pond size 5m²   Pond size 7m²

   a How many slabs would fit around a pond of size 9 square metres?
   b Write a rule to show the number of slabs needed to make a border around L-shaped ponds.

2 Write a rule to show the number of slabs needed to make a border around ponds of this shape.

3 Martha opened a post office account on Monday. She deposited £8.
On Friday, she withdrew half the money in her account.
Every Monday, she deposited £4 more than the previous Monday.
Every Friday, she withdrew half the money in her account.

   a Make a table of the amount of money in her account on the first six Saturdays.
   b Write a rule for the amount of money in her account on a Saturday.

Practice

2A Alternate and corresponding angles

1 Copy and complete these sentences.
   a *f* and ___ are alternate angles.
   b *c* and ___ are corresponding angles.
   c ___ and *a* are corresponding angles.
   d *c* and *e* are _____ angles
   e *d* and *h* are _____ angles.

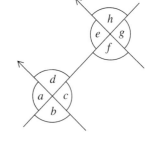

2 **a** Write down three pairs of alternate angles.
   b Write down three pairs of corresponding angles.

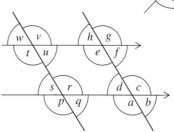

3 Copy each of these diagrams. Calculate the sizes of all the angles and mark them on your diagram.

a

b

c

d

e

f

g

h

1 **a** Find the sum of the interior angles of a nonagon.
   b Find the size of an interior angle of a *regular* nonagon.
   c Find the size of an exterior angle of a *regular* nonagon

2 Repeat Question 1, this time for a regular heptagon. Give your answers to **b** and **c** correct to 1 decimal place.

3 Calculate the size of the unknown interior angle.

a

b

c

4 Calculate the size of the unknown exterior angle.

a

b

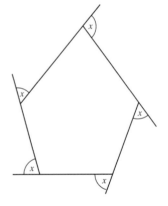

5 How many sides do these regular polygons have?

a

b

c

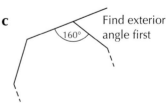

Find exterior angle first

6 For each interior angle of these regular polygons.

a **b**

  i calculate the size of the exterior angle
  ii find the number of sides the polygon has
  iii calculate the sum of its interior angles

Practice

2C Geometric proof

1 Write a proof to show that opposite
angles are equal, i.e. $a = c$ and $b = d$.
Hint: Use angles on a straight line.

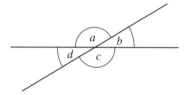

2 ABC is an isosceles triangle.
AD bisects angle A.

Write a proof to show that AD is
perpendicular to BC, i.e. $b = c = 90°$.

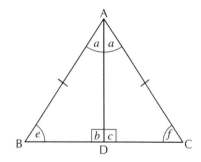

3 Write a proof to show that the opposite angles of a parallelogram are equal.

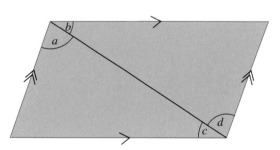

Hint: Draw a diagonal, as shown on the right.

2D The geometric properties of quadrilaterals

1 Copy this table. In each column, write the names of all possible quadrilaterals that could fit the description.

2 pairs of equal angles	Rotational symmetry of order 4	Exactly 1 line of symmetry	Exactly 2 right angles	Exactly 4 equal sides

Warning: a quadrilateral could be in more than one column!

2 A quadrilateral has two pairs of equal sides and three obtuse angles. What type of quadrilateral is it?

3 A quadrilateral has three equal angles. What type of quadrilateral could it be?

4 Which quadrilaterals have, or could have, diagonals that intersect at right angles? Illustrate your answer with drawings.

5 The diagonals of a quadrilateral divide it into four triangles. Which quadrilaterals contain at least one isosceles triangle? Illustrate your answer with drawings.

2E Constructions

1 **a** Draw a line AB, 13 cm long.
Use a ruler and compasses to bisect the line.
Check the bisection using your ruler.
b Draw another line AB 13 cm long.
Mark point C on the line, 5 cm from C.
Construct the perpendicular to AB through point C.

2 Trace this diagram.
Drop a perpendicular from point C to the line AB.

• C

A —————————————————————— B

3 Use a protractor to draw a 64° angle. Use a ruler and compasses to bisect the angle. Check the bisected angles using your protractor.

4 Repeat Question 3 for the angle 134°.

5 **a** Draw a line XY, 12 cm long.
   b Label the point 5 cm from X as point A.
   c Draw a perpendicular to XY through point A.
   d By measuring the length of the perpendicular, draw a kite with diagonals of length 12 cm and 4 cm.

6 Construct this right-angled triangle.

9.5 cm

6 cm

7 Construct a right-angled triangle with base 8 cm and height 7 cm.

8 **a** Place your outstretched hand on a sheet of paper. Mark the end of your thumb, middle finger and little finger.
   Label the points A, B and C respectively.

 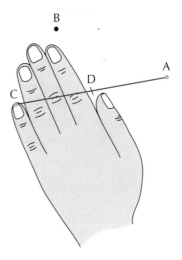

   b Draw the line AC. Bisect it using ruler and compasses.
      Label the midpoint D.
   c Compare the width of your closed hand to the length AD.
   d Drop a perpendicular from point B onto AC. Label the intersection E.

Practice

3A Probability

1 Copy this scale.

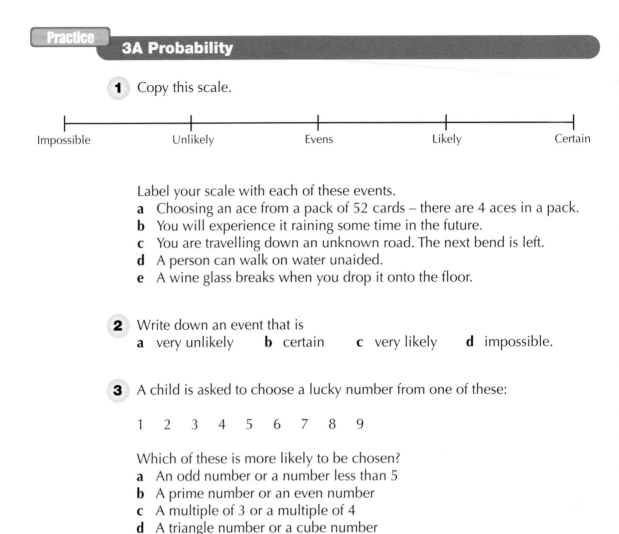

Impossible   Unlikely   Evens   Likely   Certain

Label your scale with each of these events.
a   Choosing an ace from a pack of 52 cards – there are 4 aces in a pack.
b   You will experience it raining some time in the future.
c   You are travelling down an unknown road. The next bend is left.
d   A person can walk on water unaided.
e   A wine glass breaks when you drop it onto the floor.

2 Write down an event that is
a   very unlikely   b   certain   c   very likely   d   impossible.

3 A child is asked to choose a lucky number from one of these:

1   2   3   4   5   6   7   8   9

Which of these is more likely to be chosen?
a   An odd number or a number less than 5
b   A prime number or an even number
c   A multiple of 3 or a multiple of 4
d   A triangle number or a cube number

4 Imagine these quadrilaterals are cut from plastic and placed in a bag.

rectangle   parallelogram   square   rhombus   kite   trapezium

You choose one at random.
Copy and complete these sentences by filling in the missing probability
words: impossible, very unlikely, unlikely, evens, likely, very likely, certain.
a   Picking a shape with a right angle is ___
b   Picking a shape with at least two equal sides is ___
c   Picking a shape with four equal angles is ___
d   Picking a shape with four acute angles is ___
e   Picking a shape with no equal sides is ___
f   Picking a shape with three sides is ___

1 Copy and complete this table.

Event	Probability of event occurring (p)	Probability of event *not* occurring ($1 - p$)
A	$\frac{2}{5}$	
B	0.75	
C	$\frac{5}{8}$	
D	0.12	
E	$\frac{19}{20}$	
F	0.875	
G	74%	

2 The probability of an egg having a double yoke is 0.009.
What is the probability that an egg does *not* have a double yoke?

3 100 rings are placed in a box. 20 are gold, $\frac{1}{4}$ are silver, 16 are plastic and
the rest are copper. A ring is chosen at random.
What is the probability of choosing this type of ring?

   a gold   **b** not silver   **c** copper   **d** not plastic

4 This diagram shows 12 dominoes.

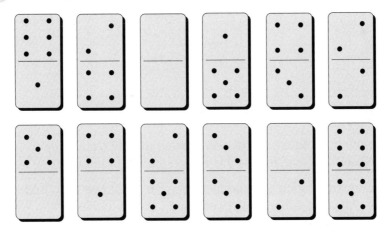

A domino is chosen at random. Calculate these probabilities.
   a It has a 5.   **b** It is a double.
   c It has a total of 7.   **d** It is *not* a double.
   e It does *not* have a 5.   **f** It does *not* have a blank.
   g It does *not* have a 3.

5 A weather forecaster estimates the probability of rain to be 35%, black ice
0.82, and a 1 in 10 chance of snow. What is the probability of

   a no snow?   **b** no black ice?   **c** no rain?

6 This matchbox cover was dropped many times.

The experimental probabilities of how it could land are shown in this table.

Landing position	Probability
Showing top	0.32
Side	0.23
End	
Showing bottom	0.3

a Calculate the probability of the matchbox cover landing
    i on end   **ii** showing its top or bottom
    iii on its side or end   **iv** not on end

b Comment on the probabilities of the matchbox cover landing on its top or bottom.

c If the box cover was dropped another 1000 times, how many times would you expect it to land showing the bottom?

Practice

3C Mutually exclusive events

1 This diagram shows diagrams of 8 faces.

Which of these pairs of events are mutually exclusive?
Note: 'Left eye' means the eye on the left of the diagram.

a A smiling face. A sad face.   **b** Left eye shut. Both eyes shut.
c Wearing a hat. Both eyes open. **d** Both eyes open. A sad face.
e Wearing a hat. Right eye shut.   **f** Smiling with an eye open. Right eye shut.

2 A six-sided dice is numbered 1, 2, 3, 3, 4, 6. It is rolled once.
Here are some events.

A number 3   **B** even number   **C** number greater than 3
D square number   **E** triangle number   **F** multiple of 3
G prime number   **H** number 1

a Write down three pairs of events that are mutually exclusive.
b Write down three pairs of events that are *not* mutually exclusive.

16

3 Two of the dice in Question 2 are rolled together.

a Make a list of the possible outcomes, e.g. (1, 6).
b What is the probability that the numbers rolled are
  i   the same, e.g. (3, 3)?   ii one odd, one even, e.g. (3, 6)?
  iii both prime, e.g. (2, 5)?   iv both multiples of 3?

3

Practice

3D Calculating probabilities

1 The letters of the word SUCCESSOR are written on card and placed in a bag. One of the cards is withdrawn from the bag.
What is the probability that the letter is

a an S?
b a vowel?
c one of the last 10 letters of the alphabet?
d a C or an S?
e a consonant?
f a letter of the word ROSE?

2 The names of two children, KIM and FRANZ, are written on cards and placed in a bag. These coins are placed in the same bag: 1p, 2p, 5p, 10p, 20p, 50p, £1. A card and a coin are taken from the bag at random. The coin is given to the named person.

a Make a table to show the possible outcomes.
b Calculate these probabilities.
  i   Kim receives 20p.
  ii   Franz receives less than 10p.
  iii One of the children receives 10p.
  iv   Kim does not receive £1.
  v   Neither child receives more than 20p.

3 A taxi firm owns a red and a green taxicab. The red taxi can carry up to six passengers. The green taxi can carry up to five passengers.

a Copy and complete this table showing the total number of passengers being carried at any one time.

		Red taxi		
		1	2	3
Green taxi	1	2		
	2			
	3			6

b What is the probability, at any one time, of these numbers of passengers being carried?

  i   7   ii   2   iii 12
  iv less than 5   v   an odd number   vi   2 or 7

1 The numbers of days it rained over different periods are recorded below.

Recording period	Number of days of rain	Experimental probability
30	12	
60	33	
100	42	
200	90	
500	235	

a Copy and complete the table.
b What is the best estimate of the probability of it raining? Explain your answer.
c Estimate the probability of it *not* raining.
d Is there a greater chance of it raining or of not raining?

2 Colour ten identical matchsticks as shown here and place them in a bag.

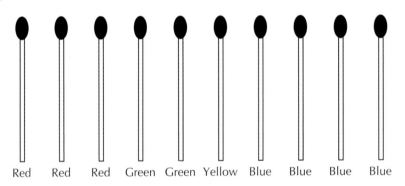

Red   Red   Red   Green   Green   Yellow   Blue   Blue   Blue   Blue

a Withdraw a matchstick from the bag and record its colour in the tally chart below. Do this 10 times.

Colour	Tally	Frequency	Experimental probability	Theoretical probability
Red				

b Calculate the experimental probabilities. Write your answers as decimals.
c Calculate the theoretical probabilities. Write your answers as decimals.
d Compare the experimental and theoretical probabilities.
e How could you make sure the experimental and theoretical probabilities are closer?
f Repeat the experiment so that the experimental and theoretical probabilities are closer.

4A Fractions and decimals

1 Write these decimals as fractions with a denominator of 10, 100 or 1000. Then cancel to their simplest form.

    a 0.6   **b** 0.36   **c** 0.65   **d** 0.255   **e** 0.025

2 *Without* using a calculator, convert these fractions to decimals.

    a $\frac{13}{50}$ **b** $\frac{17}{25}$ **c** $\frac{4}{5}$ **d** $\frac{3}{20}$

3 Which of these fractions have recurring decimals? Try to answer the questions without using a calculator. Then check to see if you are correct.

    a $\frac{3}{8}$ **b** $\frac{2}{7}$ **c** $\frac{9}{25}$ **d** $\frac{13}{40}$ **e** $\frac{5}{6}$

    f $\frac{19}{50}$ **g** $\frac{4}{9}$ **h** $\frac{3}{14}$ **i** $\frac{15}{16}$ **j** $\frac{16}{21}$

4 Find the larger of each pair of fractions.

    a $\frac{3}{25}$ and $\frac{1}{7}$ **b** $\frac{11}{18}$ and $\frac{9}{16}$ **c** $\frac{7}{11}$ and $\frac{29}{40}$

5 Write these fractions in increasing order of size.

    $\frac{5}{7}, \frac{13}{16}, \frac{33}{50}, \frac{22}{27}$

6 **a** Calculate $\frac{2}{9}$ using your calculator. Describe the display on your calculator.

    b Calculate $\frac{24}{99}$ using your calculator. Describe the display on your calculator.

    c Find fractions that give these calculator displays.

        i 0.888888888   **ii** 0.737373737   **iii** 0.657657657

        iv 0.123412341   **v** 0.044444444   **vi** 0.036363636

        vii 0.020202020   **viii** 0.002828282

4B Adding and subtracting fractions

1 Find the lowest common multiple of each of these pairs of numbers.

    a 2, 5   **b** 6, 8   **c** 2, 6   **d** 10, 15   **e** 9, 12

For Questions 2–4 convert to equivalent fractions with a common denominator. Then work out the answer. Cancel your answers and write them as mixed numbers if necessary.

2 **a** $\frac{2}{5} + \frac{1}{2}$ **b** $\frac{5}{8} + \frac{1}{12}$ **c** $\frac{3}{5} - \frac{1}{2}$ **d** $\frac{5}{9} - \frac{1}{6}$ **e** $\frac{3}{7} + \frac{2}{3}$

    f $\frac{5}{12} + \frac{1}{8}$ **g** $\frac{3}{5} + \frac{1}{2} + \frac{7}{10}$ **h** $\frac{7}{9} - \frac{1}{2}$ **i** $\frac{11}{15} - \frac{2}{5}$ **j** $\frac{2}{3} + \frac{5}{6} - \frac{5}{12}$

3 a $2\frac{1}{5} - \frac{7}{10}$ b $1\frac{3}{4} + \frac{5}{6}$ c $3\frac{1}{8} - 2\frac{2}{3}$ d $4\frac{1}{10} - 2\frac{1}{4}$

4 a $\frac{11}{18} - \frac{7}{24}$ b $\frac{19}{40} + \frac{43}{60}$ c $2\frac{3}{25} + 4\frac{7}{10}$ d $8\frac{3}{16} - 5\frac{11}{12}$

5 Calculate these.

a $\frac{4}{9}$ of 36 kg b $\frac{5}{12}$ of 600 ml c $\frac{2}{7}$ of 98 cm

6 Work out these. Cancel your answers and write them as mixed numbers if necessary.

a $4 \times \frac{3}{7}$ b $9 \times \frac{5}{6}$ c $\frac{2}{5} \div 3$ d $\frac{8}{9} \div 6$

7 a $3\frac{3}{4}$ cakes were shared equally among 12 people.
What fraction of a cake did each person receive?

b Kailash measured the length and breadth of this picture frame he made.

i   What is the total length of frame material used?

ii Kailash has 50 inches of frame material to make an identical frame.
How much frame material will be left over?

iii He bought a 97-inch strip of frame material. How many of the above frames could he make from it?
Show your working.

Practice

4C Percentages

1 Without using a calculator, express

a 19 as a percentage of 25 b 13 as a percentage of 20
c 96 as a percentage of 400 d 3 as a percentage of 50

2 Use a calculator to express, correct to the nearest per cent,

a 14 as a percentage of 23 b 81 as a percentage of 120
c 6 as a percentage of 65 d 3200 as a percentage of 7000

3 Milton drinks 35 cl of an 80-cl bottle of orange.

a What percentage did he drink? b What percentage remains?

4 A company employs 280 workers. At the last general election, 130 voted Labour, 83 voted Liberal Democrat and the remainder voted Conservative. Calculate the percentage vote for each party.

5 Three people contributed £23, £18.50 and £25.60 toward their total restaurant bill. What percentage of the total bill did each person contribute?

6 **a** Stuart took a maths test lasting 80 minutes. He spent 23 minutes on the Algebra section, 33 minutes on the Number section and the remaining time on the Shape and Space section.
What percentage of the time did he spend on each section?

b Marcel spent the same amount of time on each section as Stuart. But he also took an Extension section lasting 30 minutes.
What percentage of the time did he spend on each section?

4D Percentage increase and decrease

Do not use a calculator for Questions 1–4.

1 Calculate

    a 70% of 300 cm   **b** 5% of £30
    c 35% of 4000 kg   **d** 85% of 8 inches

2 **a** Increase $40 by 20%.   **b** Decrease 200 kg by 5%.
    c Decrease 7p by 60%.   **d** Increase 2000 m by 95%.
    e Increase 230 ml by 45%.   **f** Decrease £7.60 by 85%.

3 **a** Before a typing course, Leon could type 60 words per minute.
The typing course increased his speed by 35%.
What was his speed after the course?

    b Leon injured his hand, reducing his speed by 20%.
What is his speed now?

4 Three people each withdrew a certain percentage of their bank balance from their bank account.

    John 29% of £300

    Hans 75% of £640

    Will 15% of £280

Which person has the largest remaining bank balance?

Use a calculator for Questions 5–9.

5 Calculate

    a 34% of $45   **b** 89% of £33 290
    c 17 1/2% of £90   **d** 5 1/2% of 9 000 000 tons
    e 52.9% of 700 litres   **f** 2.1% of £5300

6 **a** Increase 254 cm^2 by 18%.   **b** Decrease £15.23 by 84%.
    c Increase 7000 g by 47.2%.   **d** Increase 0.74 litres by 31%.
    e Decrease £17 400 by 97%.   **f** Decrease 900 cm by 2.8%.

7 A coat costs £72 before VAT of 17.5% is added.
What is the price including VAT?

8 Marvin's average score on the computer game Space Attack was 256.

  a After buying a new gamepad, his average score increased by 28%.
  What was his new average score, to the nearest whole number?

  b Marvin went on holiday. When he returned, his average score had
  decreased by 15%.
  What was his new average score, to the nearest whole number?

9 'Zipping' a computer files reduces its size by a certain percentage.
Find the size of each file after zipping.

  a 500 kB file reduced by 17%   **b** 740 kB file reduced by 43%
  c 655 kB file reduced by 23%   **d** 1200 kB file reduced by 69.2%

Practice

4E Real-life problems

1 Marcia has an annual salary of £24 000. Her tax allowance is £4800.
She pays 10% on the first £1880 of her taxable income.
She pays 22% tax on the remaining taxable income.

  a How much tax does she pay altogether?
  b How much of her annual salary does she receive?
  c What is her monthly income?
  d She pays 3% of the salary she received toward a pension scheme.
  How much is this?
  e In 2003, she received a 7% increase in her annual salary. Her tax
  allowance remained the same. Recalculate the answers to parts **a** to **d**.

2 Mrs Walker left £45 750 in her will. The money was to be divided between
her three children:

  Derek 37%   Maria 29%   Jason 34%

The solicitors deducted 6% for expenses. The remainder was divided among
the children. How much did each child receive?

3 Three dealers offer these repayment options for a car with a marked price
of £12 600.

Trustworthy Cars   20% deposit followed by 12 monthly payments of £900
Bargain Autos   114% of the marked price spread over 18 months
Future Car Sales   7% of the marked price for each of the first 6 months
                    followed by 6 monthly payments of £1300

Which deal works out the cheapest overall?

4 Amanda deposited £3000 in her bank. She kept the money in the bank for
5 years. The bank paid interest of 4% per annum. Calculate the amount of
interest Amanda received after 5 years if she

  a spends the interest at the end of each year
  b adds the interest to her bank account at the end of each year.

Hint: Work out the amount in her account at the end of Year 1, then Year 2
and so on.

CHAPTER 5

Algebra 2

5A Algebraic shorthand

1 Write each of these expressions using algebraic shorthand.

a $x \div 5$ **b** $3 \times b$ **c** $4 \times m \times n$

d $p \div q$ **e** $2 \times (x - 1)$ **f** $5 \times m + 3$

g $c \div (d + 2)$ **h** $5 \times t \div 4$ **i** $(a + b) \times (m - n)$

2 Simplify these expressions.

a $6n \times t$ **b** $5k \times 3m$ **c** $h \times 5g$ **d** $2u \times 3t \times 4v$

3 Simplify these expressions.

a $4x \div 4$ **b** $\dfrac{9y}{9}$ **c** $\dfrac{8a}{2}$ **d** $\dfrac{7b}{b}$ **e** $\dfrac{20i}{5i}$

4 Solve each of these equations.
In your solution, write each equation on a separate line.

a $5x + 7 = 22$ **b** $2p - 9 = 7$ **c** $10m + 15 = 125$

d $12c - 13 = 71$ **e** $4k + 8 = 19$ **f** $8f - 25 = 98$

5 Which of these statements are incorrect?
If you are unsure, check by substituting a number for the letter.

a $6 \div d$ is the same as $\dfrac{d}{6}$

b $4(a + 2)$ is the same as $2(a + 4)$

c $\dfrac{10m}{5}$ is the same as $2m$

d $\dfrac{12}{3n}$ is the same as $4n$

e $(a - 2) \div 2$ is the same as $2 \times (a + 2)$

f $6 \times d \div 2$ is the same as $\dfrac{6d}{2}$

6 Which of these statements are incorrect?

a $5 \times p = 12$ is the same as $12 = 5p$

b $5m + 2 = 17$ is the same as $17 = 5m + 2$

c $9 = 2j - 4$ is the same as $2j + 4 = 9$

d $n + 3 = 12$ is the same as $12 = 3 + n$

e $2t + 3 = 9$ is the same as $3 = 2t + 9$

f $7 - 3p = 10$ is the same as $10 = 3p - 7$

7 Write down the equivalent expressions, e.g. $5d = 5 \times d = d5$.

$st + 3$

$3 - st$

$3s + t$

$3 + t \times s$

$3 \div s + t$ $3 + st$

$3 \times s \times t$

$ts - 3$ $s \times 3 + t$

$t + s3$ $t \times 3 + s$

$\frac{s}{3} + t$ $s3t$

$s + 3t$

$t + \frac{3}{s}$ $t \times s + 3$

Practice

5B Like terms

1 Make a list of the terms in each of these.

   a $y + 2x - 3$ **b** $4x = 3 + 2x$ **c** $\frac{4}{t} - u$ **d** $3x^2 = 14x + 2$

For Questions 2–5, simplify the expressions.

2 **a** $4i + 7i$ **b** $7r - 2r$ **c** $-u - u$
   d $3h + 2h - h$ **e** $6y - 8y$ **f** $-3m + 5m$
   g $4t - 3t - 6t$ **h** $4n - 3n$ **i** $5zt + 4zt$
   j $-ab - ab$ **k** $2ad + 7ad - 10ad$ **l** $3f^2 - f^2$

3 **a** $6k + 4k + 3l$ **b** $7h + 3i - 2i$ **c** $10y + 2x + 3y$
   d $4p + 2p - 1$ **e** $4d - 7d + 2e$ **f** $7t - 2u - 4t$
   g $9w + 3x - 10w$ **h** $3fg + 7f + 2fg$ **i** $s^2 - t^2 + 3s^2$

4 **a** $4q + 3q + 6i + i$ **b** $8z - 3z + 4b - 2b$
   c $9u + 3v + 2u + 4v$ **d** $7j + 5k - 3k + 2j$
   e $3m - 5m - 4n + 7n$ **f** $4d + 6e - 8e + 2d$
   g $-3c + 4d + 8c - 5d$ **h** $10r - 4s - 7s - 8r$
   i $g - h - 2g + 2h$

5 **a** $2m^2 + m^2 + 4m - m$ **b** $5h^2 + 3h + 7h - 3h^2$
   c $2p^2 + 6p + 4p^2 - 4p$ **d** $8d^2 - 3d - 5d^2 - 2d$

Practice

5C Expanding brackets and factorising

1 Expand the brackets.

   a $2(f + k)$ **b** $s(t - 4)$ **c** $4(2a + 3)$ **d** $m(n + 3r)$
   e $3(3w - 2s)$ **f** $a(2b - 3)$ **g** $5(s + t - u)$ **h** $d(2 - 3r + 4g)$

2 Expand the brackets.

    a $-(p + q)$ **b** $-(3r - s)$ **c** $-4(a + b)$ **d** $-2(m - n)$ **e** $-5(2d - 3e)$

For Questions 3–6, expand and simplify the expressions.

3 **a** $4(f + g) + 6f$ **b** $2k + 3(3k - s)$ **c** $4x + 2(2y - 3x)$

4 **a** $5(p + q) + 2(2p + 3q)$ **b** $4(2i + j) + 3(i - j)$
      c $2(3b - 2a) + 4(b - 2a)$ **d** $5(m - 3n) + 2(3m + 4n)$

5 **a** $4t - (2t + 3u)$ **b** $7m - (2m - n)$ **c** $2x - (4y + 3x)$

6 **a** $4(h + i) - (2h + 3i)$ **b** $6(2s + t) - (3s - 2t)$
      c $5(2w - v) - 3(4w + 2v)$

7 Factorise these expressions by filling in the boxes.

    a $10m - 8 = \boxed{}(5m - 4)$

    b $12d + 8e = 4(\boxed{} + \boxed{})$

    c $st + 4s = \boxed{}(t + 4)$

    d $5de - 2e = e(\boxed{} - \boxed{})$

    e $2n + 6 = \boxed{}(\boxed{} + \boxed{})$

    f $14sf - 7 = \boxed{}(\boxed{} - \boxed{})$

    g $t - ty = \boxed{}(\boxed{} - \boxed{})$

    h $3mh + 5nh = \boxed{}(\boxed{} + \boxed{})$

8 Factorise these expressions.

    a $6f + 9$ **b** $8 - 4s$ **c** $df + de$ **d** $6ab - 5a$
    e $12v^2 - 8$ **f** $8w - 2$ **g** $rt - r$ **h** $15st - 10$

Practice

5D Using algebra and shapes

1 Write down the perimeter and area of each shape as simply as possible.

a

5 (height), $2x - 1$ (base)

b

3 (height), $4n + 1$ (base)

c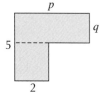

p, q, 5, 2

d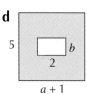

5, b, 2, $a + 1$

e

6, $m + 1$, 2, $m - 2$

2 a Write down the area of the large parallelogram.

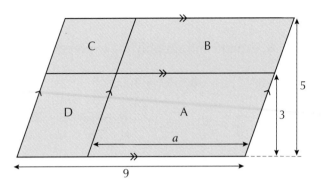

b Write down the areas of the smaller parallelograms, A to D.
c Show that the sum of the smaller areas is the same as your answer to part **a**.

3 For each question, mark any necessary lengths on your diagram.

a Sketch a rectangle whose area is abc.
b Sketch a rectangle whose perimeter is $6x + 4y$.
c Sketch a triangle whose area is $8x$.
d Sketch a rectangle whose area is $5x + 10$.

Practice

5E Index notation with algebra

1 Write these expressions using index form.

a $g \times g \times g \times g \times g \times g$ **b** $9k \times k$ **c** $5t \times 3t$
d $r \times 4r$ **e** $2j \times 2j \times 2j$

2 Write these expressions as briefly as possible.

a $m + m + m + m + m + m + m + m$
b $t \times t \times t \times t \times t$ **c** $d + d + d + e \times e \times e$

3 Show the difference between $6w$ and w^6.

4 Expand the brackets.

a $v(3 + v)$ **b** $m(3m - 2n)$ **c** $D(3E - 2D)$ **d** $3s(2s + 3t)$

5 Expand and simplify these expressions.

a $2ab + a(3b + 2)$ **b** $v(2v + 4t) - 2vt$ **c** $9qz - q(3z - 2q)$

6 Expand and simplify these expressions.

a $r(2r + s) + s(3r + s)$ **b** $p(3p - 2q) + q(4p - 5q)$
b $m(3m + 2n) - n(2m + 4n)$ **c** $c(3c - 2d) - d(5c - d)$

7 Expand and simplify these expressions.

    a $2g^2 + g(3g + 4)$ **b** $d(2d + 4e) + d(3d - e)$

    c $w(4 - 2w) + w(4w + 3)$

8 Simplify

    a $d^2 \times d^4$ **b** hh^3 **c** $2m \times 5m^4$ **d** $3a^3 \times 4a^2$

    e $\dfrac{u^5}{u}$ **f** $n^7 \div n^2$ **g** $\dfrac{14u^6}{7u^2}$ **h** $20v^8 \div 4v^3$

9 Expand and simplify

    a $d(d^2 + 2d) + d(3d + 4)$ **b** $4c(c^2 - 3) + 2c^2(c + 5)$

10 Factorise

    a $r^2 + 4r$ **b** $5s^2 - 2s$ **c** $a^2b + 3a$ **d** $a^3 - a$ **e** $4w - 5w^3$

CHAPTER 6   Shape, Space and Measures 2

Practice

6A The circle

1 **a** Name the lines on this diagram.

    i AB   **ii** AC

    iii DE   **iv** CF

    v CG

    b Name these shapes.

    i ABCA   **ii** ACFA

    iii ABCFA   **iv** GABCG

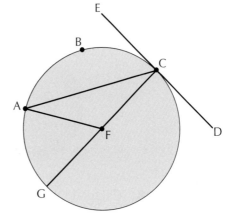

2 **a** Measure the diameter of a bicycle wheel to the nearest centimetre.

    b Measure the circumference of the wheel by rolling it along the ground for one turn.

    c Use a calculator to divide your answer to **b** by your answer to **a**.

    d The answer should be a little more than 3. How much more?

1 Use the approximation $\pi \approx 3.14$ to calculate the circumference of each wheel. Write your answers correct to the nearest centimetre.

a

60 cm

b

17.2 cm

2 Use the π button of your calculator to calculate the circumference of each coaster. Write your answers correct to 1 decimal place.

a

10 cm

b

3.5 cm

3 Use the approximation $\pi \approx \frac{22}{7}$ to calculate the circumference of each coin. Do not use a calculator.

a

TWO POUNDS

14 mm

1998

b

Car wash coin

21 mm

4 Calculate the total length of the lines in this crop circle. It has two semicircles, a circle and straight lines. Write your answers correct to the nearest centimetre.

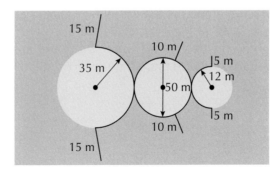

15 m

10 m

5 m

35 m

12 m

50 m

10 m

5 m

15 m

Use the approximation π ≈ 3.14 or the π button of your calculator for
these questions.

1 Calculate the area of the lid of each tin. Write your answers using a suitable
degree of accuracy.

a

b

c

2 Calculate the total area of this
arched window.
Write your answer correct to the
nearest square centimetre.

3 This diagram shows how a washer is made.

a Calculate the area of the blank, correct to 1 decimal place.
b Calculate the area of the hole, correct to 1 decimal place.
c Calculate the area of the finished washer, correct to the nearest mm^2.

Blank

Centre removed

Finished washer

1 Convert these quantities.

   a $0.07\,\text{m}^2$ to cm^2 **b** $8400\,\text{cm}^3$ to l   **c** $21\,000\,000\,\text{cm}^3$ to m^3

   d $4.8\,\text{ml}$ to mm^3 **e** $5340\,\text{mm}^2$ to cm^2 **f** 5200 l to m^3

2 **i** Calculate the surface area of each prism.

   ii Calculate the volume of each prism.

a

8 cm

12 cm

3 cm

b

25 mm

5 mm

12 mm

13 mm

3 Convert your answers to Question **2b** to cm^2 and cm^3.

4 The cross-section of this plastic
bench has an area of $620\,\text{cm}^2$.
Calculate its volume in
a cm^3 and **b** m^3.

1.8 m

5 The diagram shows a petrol tank in the shape of a prism.

50 cm

13 cm

12 cm

40 cm

80 cm

   a Calculate the area of the cross-section.

   b Calculate the volume of the tank.

   c Calculate the capacity of the tank in litres.

   d Calculate the surface area of the tank in m^2.

1 Convert each of these quantities to the units shown in brackets.

    a 25 st (lb)   **b** 7 miles (yd)   **c** 9 ft 7 in (in)   **d** $3\frac{1}{2}$ ton (lb)

2 Convert each of these quantities to the units shown in brackets.

    a 83 oz (lb and oz)   **b** 532 ft (yd and ft)
    c 75 pt (gall and pt)   **d** 125 in (ft and in)

3   **a** How many stones are in a ton?
    b How many feet are in a mile?

4 Convert each Imperial quantity to the approximate metric quantity shown in brackets. Use 1 oz ≈ 30 g and 1 lb ≈ 450 g.

    a 11 oz (g)   **b** 270 miles (km)
    c 100 in (m)   **d** $7\frac{1}{4}$ lb (kg)

5 Convert each metric quantity to the approximate Imperial quantity shown in brackets.

    a 72 km (miles)   **b** 420 g (oz)
    c 81 l (gall and pt)   **d** 720 g (lb and oz)

6 Calculate the approximate length of this tape measure in yards, feet and inches.

Use the approximation 1 in ≈ 2.5 cm.

TAPE MEASURE

16 metres

7 A small Dutch beer glass holds 0.25 l of beer. How many pints does it hold?

8 Convert this recipe to Imperial units.

Biscuits

750g plain flour
360g butter
315g sugar
75g rice flour
15g salt

9 You know that 1 in ≈ 2.5 cm and 1 oz ≈ 30 g.
Find a close metric approximation (shown in brackets) for each of these.

    a 1 yd (cm)   **b** 1 lb (g)   **c** 1 mile (m)

7A Linear functions

1 **a** Copy this mapping diagram.

   b For the function $x \to x - 3$, map the integer values from $x = -1$ to $x = 4$.
   c Map these integer values.

   i $x = 3.5$ **ii** $x = 0.5$
   iii $x = 1.5$ **iv** $x = -0.5$

2 **a** For each of these functions, draw a mapping diagram using two lines from $x = -5$ to $x = 10$. Label your diagrams.

   i $x \to x + 3$ **ii** $x \to x - 1$ **iii** $x \to 2x$
   iv $x \to 2x + 4$ **v** $x \to 2x - 2$ **vi** $x \to 3x + 3$

   b Map these integer values.

   i $x = 2.5$ **ii** $x = 0.5$
   iii $x = -1.5$ **iv** $x = -0.5$

3 Draw a mapping diagram for the function $x \to -2x$ using two number lines from $x = -6$ to $x = 6$.

7B Finding functions from inputs and outputs

For Questions 1–4, find the function that maps the inputs to the outputs.

1 **a** $\{1, 2, 3, 4, 5\} \to \{7, 8, 9, 10, 11\}$
   b $\{3, 4, 5, 6, 7\} \to \{6, 8, 10, 12, 14\}$
   c $\{0, 1, 2, 3, 4\} \to \{-2, -1, 0, 1, 2\}$
   d $\{1, 2, 3, 4, 5\} \to \{3, 5, 7, 9, 11\}$
   e $\{2, 3, 4, 5, 6\} \to \{5, 8, 11, 14, 17\}$
   f $\{-2, -1, 0, 1, 2\} \to \{1, 3, 5, 7, 9\}$
   g $\{-1, 0, 1, 2, 3\} \to \{-6, -2, 2, 6, 10\}$

2 **a** $\{3, 4, 5, 8, 9\} \to \{8, 11, 14, 23, 26\}$
   b $\{2, 4, 5, 6, 8\} \to \{8, 14, 17, 20, 26\}$
   c $\{0, 4, 6, 7, 8\} \to \{-3, 17, 27, 32, 37\}$
   d $\{1, 3, 5, 7, 9\} \to \{4, 12, 20, 28, 36\}$
   e $\{3, 6, 9, 12, 15\} \to \{3, 9, 15, 21, 27\}$

3 a {3, 1, 2, 5, 4} → {12, 4, 8, 20, 16}
   b {6, 0, 3, 2, 1} → {13, 1, 7, 5, 3}
   c {4, 2, 5, 3, 6} → {22, 16, 25, 19, 28}
   Hint: Rearrange the inputs and outputs in sequence first.

4 a {1, 2} → {5, 7}   b   {2, 4} → {4, 10}   c   {0, 3} → {1, 16}

5 For each function
   i   find the outputs for the inputs {1, 2, 3, 4, 5}
   ii find the inverse of the function
   iii check that the inverse function maps the outputs of **i** to the
        inputs given.
   a $x \rightarrow x + 5$ b $x \rightarrow 6x$ c $x \rightarrow 2x - 3$ d $x \rightarrow 4x + 5$

7C Graphs of functions

1 a Copy and complete this table for the function $y = 4x - 3$.

x	0	1	2	3	4	5
$y = 4x - 3$						

   b Draw a grid with its x-axis from 0 to 5 and y-axis from –5 to 20.
   c Draw the graph of the function $y = 4x - 3$.

2 a Copy and complete this table.

x	–2	–1	0	1	2	3
$y = x + 2$						
$y = 2x + 2$						
$y = 3x + 2$						
$y = 4x + 2$						

   b Draw a grid with its x-axis from –2 to 3 and y-axis from –10 to 15.
   c Draw the graph of each function in the table.
   d What is the same about the lines?
   e What is different about the lines?
   f Use a dotted line to sketch the graph of $y = 2.5x + 2$.

3 For the function $8y + 6x = 24$
   a find y when $x = 0$
   b find x when $y = 0$
   c find a third point that lies on the line
   d draw the graph of the function.

4 Draw the graph of the function $10y + 4x = 20$ by finding three points that
   lie on the line.

1 Find the gradient of each of these lines.

a

b

c

d

2 Find the equation of each line in Question 1.

3 **a** Draw five lines that pass through the point (1, 3).
   b For each line
      i find the gradient
      ii find where it cuts the *y*-axis
      iii write down its equation

4 For each function
   i state the gradient
   ii state the *y*-intercept
   iii draw a graph using squared paper (do not plot any points other than the *y*-intercept)
   a $y = 3x + 5$ **b** $y = 2x - 2$

1 **a** Copy this grid.

Mrs Jay's journey for a job interview

b Draw on your grid a distance–time graph for Mrs Jay's train journey. Mark the places she visited on the vertical axis.

Mrs Jay had to travel to a job interview at Penford. She caught the 0900 train from Shobton and travelled to Deely 30 miles away in an hour. There she had to wait 30 minutes for a connecting train to Penford. This part of the journey took $1\frac{1}{2}$ hours at a speed of 60 mph. Her job interview at Penford lasted 2 hours. Her return journey lasted $1\frac{1}{2}$ hours.

c Calculate the average speed of the train on her return journey.

2 a Draw a grid with these scales:
horizontal axis represents time, from 0 to 6 hours, 1 cm to 30 minutes
vertical axis represents distance from factory, from 0 to 50 miles, 1 cm to 5 miles.

b Draw on the grid a distance–time graph for the lorry journey. Mark the places of delivery on the vertical axis.

A car transporter left the factory and took 30 minutes to travel 15 miles to a dealer in Harton. It took half an hour to unload three of the cars. The transporter travelled at 25 mph for another hour and made a delivery at Glimp. This delivery and lunch took an hour. A final delivery was made 30 minutes later at Unwich after a 10-mile drive. This delivery took 30 minutes. The transporter returned to the factory at a speed of 50 mph.

c Calculate the average speed of the transporter
   i between Glimp and Unwich   **ii** on the return journey.

3 a Draw a grid with these scales:
horizontal axis represents time, from 0 to 30 minutes, 1 cm to 2 minutes
vertical axis represents temperature, from 20°C to 100°C, 1 cm to 10°C

b Draw a graph on the grid to show the temperature of Stan's CupSoup. Stan's microwave takes 4 minutes to boil a mug of CupSoup at full power. He left the mug in the microwave on full power for 6 minutes. He forgot about the soup for a further 9 minutes, by which time it had cooled to 80°C. So he heated it to boiling point on quarter power. It took him 9 minutes to eat the soup. The temperature of the last spoonful was 50°C.

CHAPTER 8 Number 3

Practice

8A Powers of 10

Do not use your calculator.

1 Round these numbers **i** to 1 decimal place and **ii** to 2 decimal places.
   a 8.265   **b** 3.965   **c** 0.047
   d 4.994   **e** 0.095

2 Multiply each of these numbers by 10^4.

    a 2.7   **b** 0.05   **c** 38   **d** 0.008

3 Divide each of these numbers by 10^3.

    a 730   **b** 4   **c** 2.8   **d** 35 842

4 Calculate these.

    a 7.4×10^3 **b** 13×10^5 **c** $0.87 \div 10^3$

    d $17.4 \div 10^2$ **e** 0.0065×10^3 **f** $19.4 \div 10^4$

5 Multiply these numbers **i** by 0.01 and **ii** by 0.001.

    a 280   **b** 0.6

    c 1.05   **d** 9851

6 Divide these numbers **i** by 0.01 and **ii** by 0.001.

    a 4   **b** 800   **c** 0.9   **d** 67.2

7 Work your way along this chain of calculations for each of these starting numbers.

    a 2000   **b** 7   **c** 0.6

$\times 10^2$ $\div 10^3$ $\times 0.001$ $\div 0.01$ $\times 10^4$ $\div 0.1$ $\div 10^5$

8B Rounding

1 Write these numbers in words.

    a 956 348   **b** 15 230 421

    c 8002 040   **d** 604 500 002

2 Write these numbers using figures.

    a Two hundred and six thousand, one hundred and seven

    b Fifty million, thirty-two thousand and eight

3 This graph shows the numbers of a company's shares sold every hour during a trading day.

Estimate the number sold each hour. Make a table for your answers.

4 Round these numbers
   i to the nearest ten thousand
   ii to the nearest hundred thousand
   iii to the nearest nearest million.
   a 7247 964   **b** 1952 599   **c** 645 491   **d** 9595 902

5 This table shows the top coal producers in 1996.

Country	Coal production (tons)
China	1328 670 000
USA	948 965 640
India	303 133 600
Russia	250 971 000
Australia	246 050 000
Germany	231 385 420

A billion is 1000 million (1000 000 000).

a *Energy World* magazine stated that the USA produced a billion tons of coal in 1996. Are they correct?
b Which countries produced the same amount of coal to the nearest hundred million tons?
c What is the total production of these countries, to the nearest billion?

6 Use a calculator to find these values.
   a 10^{-5} **b** 10^{-8} **c** 9×10^{-3}
   d 230×10^{-4} **e** 0.52×10^{-1}

8C Estimations

1 Estimate each value pointed to by the arrows.

a
0   4.8

b
0   9.2

c
−10   10

2 Estimate answers to these.

a 71% of £589   b √80   c 33 × 777

d 7.57²   e ⅕ of 973   f 274 ÷ 53

g $\frac{34.9 + 73.8}{62.8 - 38.9}$ h 0.745 × 0.328   i 2.502 ÷ 0.0483

3 Choose the closest answer in the brackets. Justify your choice.

a 35.82 × 73.29 (2350, 280, 2740)

b 0.834² (0.92, 0.06, 0.64)

c √60 (8.3, 6.9, 7.7)

4 Which of these statements is likely to be correct? Explain your answer using estimation and number facts.

a 34% of 69 = 22

b 4.55 is halfway between 3.109 and 8.691

c ⅕ of 1620 = 323

d Thirty-nine 0.23 kg bags of salt weigh 18 kg, to the nearest kilogram.

Practice

8D Working with decimals

Do not use a calculator, apart from Questions 2 and 10. Show your working.

1 Round these numbers **i** to 2 decimal places and **ii** to 3 decimal places.

a 7.5745   b 40.595 99   c 0.039 493

d 8.899 99   e 126.039 555

2 Work out these using a calculator. Write your answers correct to 3 decimal places.

a 1200 ÷ 2893   b 0.342²   c √5   d $\frac{1}{32.4 - 4.3^2}$

3 Calculate these.

    a 2.06 + 9.77 + 12.3   **b** 0.87 + 1.79 − 0.94

    c 78.008 − 23.7 − 19.08   **d** 9.231 − 2.076 − 1.8

    e 13 + 91.03 − 2.378 − 18.26 + 33.333

4 Calculate these. Work in metres.

    a 5 m − 2.56 m + 108 cm   **b** 0.95 m + 239 cm − 1.86 m

    c 6 cm + 0.67 m − 0.085 m   **d** 23.6 cm + 0.082 m − 7.41 cm

5 **a** Calculate the total volume of juice in these full bottles. Work in litres.
      Remember: 1 litre = 100 cl = 1000 ml.

    b All the juice is made into a fruit cocktail. Three cups are drunk.
        If a cup holds 15.3 cl, how much fruit cocktail is left?

6 The skin is the largest organ in the body and weighs 10.886 kg, on average.
    The four other largest organs are Liver 1.56 kg, Brain 1.408 kg, Lungs
    1.09 kg, Heart 0.315 kg.

    a Calculate the total weight of these organs.

    b How much more does the skin weigh compared to the total weight of
        the other organs?

7 A candle is 32.7 cm tall. It burns down 18.4 mm each day.
    What is its height at the end of 4 days? Work in centimetres.

8 1 kilobyte (kB) of computer information ≈ 1000 bytes

    a Calculate the total size of these computer files: 375.2 kB, 973 bytes,
        1.867 kB, 2854 bytes, 66 bytes. Work in kilobytes.

    b The files are stored on a blank floppy disk of size 1440 kB.
        How much space is left on the disk?

9 Calculate the area of each of these shapes, giving your answers correct to 3 decimal places.

a   **b**   **c**

6.235 m

6.235 m

0.73 cm

0.58 cm

0.141 mm

0.057 mm

0.203 mm

10   **a**   Use a calculator to find the value of $\sqrt{2}$ correct to 8 decimal places.

     b   Which of these fractions gives the closest approximation to $\sqrt{2}$? Show your working.

       i $\frac{71}{50}$ **ii** $\frac{482}{341}$ **iii** $\frac{3542}{2503}$ **iv** $\frac{10\,600}{7499}$

Practice

8E Efficient calculations

1   Use the bracket and/or memory keys on your calculator to calculate these.

     a $19.3 - (32.5 - 24.8)$ **b** $(0.24 + 1.73)^2$ **c** $\dfrac{1}{2.09 - 1.93}$

2   Use the fraction key on your calculator to calculate these.

     a $\frac{7}{9} - \frac{1}{6}$ **b** $2\frac{3}{5} + 7\frac{1}{4}$ **c** $9\frac{3}{10} \times 2\frac{1}{2}$

     d $1\frac{3}{8} \div \left(\frac{5}{6} - \frac{2}{9}\right)$ **e** $\left(5\frac{1}{4} - 2\frac{1}{7}\right)^2$ **f** $\dfrac{3\frac{5}{8} - 2\frac{2}{3}}{4\frac{1}{6} + 3\frac{1}{2}}$

3   Use the power, cube and cube root keys on your calculator to calculate these. Round your answers to 1 decimal place if necessary.

     a 3^7 **b** $\sqrt[3]{29}$ **c** $9.8^2 \times 2.5$

     d $14^2 \div 15^2$ **e** $\sqrt{1 + 1.8^3}$

4   Solve each of these problems using the fraction key of your calculator.

     a   A wheel turns seventeen $\frac{1}{4}$ turns clockwise, then three $\frac{2}{5}$ turns anticlockwise, then seven $\frac{2}{3}$ turns clockwise. How far has it turned altogether?

b A cat eats $\frac{2}{5}$ of a tin of cat food every day. How long would $5\frac{1}{2}$ tins last?

c Salami costs £8.58 per kilogram. How much does $3\frac{3}{8}$ kg cost?

d A giant company Christmas cake is cut into six equal parts. Two-fifths of one part is divided between eight office staff.

   i What fraction of the cake does each person receive?
     The remaining cake is divided between twenty-five factory workers.

   ii What fraction of the cake does each factory worker receive?

   iii What is the difference between the amount received by an office worker and a factory worker?

Practice

8F Multiplying and dividing decimals

Do not use a calculator.

1 Calculate these.

  a 0.3×0.9 **b** 1.7×0.8 **c** 0.7×0.04
  d 0.08×0.08 **e** 5.2×9.3 **f** 3.8×6.6
  g 4.31×2.7 **h** 0.49×0.78

2 Calculate these.

  a $6 \div 0.3$ **b** $12 \div 0.04$ **c** $0.8 \div 0.02$
  d $1.8 \div 0.06$ **e** $2.16 \div 0.4$ **f** $0.24 \div 1.6$
  g $29.9 \div 23$ **h** $1.12 \div 0.35$

3 Bricks are 23.7 cm long. How far would 17 bricks reach laid end to end?

4 The table shows the postage needed for letters.

Weight up to	First class	Second class
60 g	£0.27	£0.19
100 g	£0.41	£0.33
150 g	£0.57	£0.44

Answer these questions by working in decimals.

a What is the cost of sending 14 letters weighing 120 g by first class mail?

b How many second class 45 g letters could be posted for £3.04?

c Which is cheaper to post: 18 first class 130 g letters or 26 second class 85 g letters?

d Which is the greater number of stamps: £9.18 worth of first class stamps for 50 g letters or £13.64 worth of second class stamps for 105 g letters?

9A Congruent shapes

1 Use your ruler to check which of these triangles are congruent. Write your answer like this, e.g. A = D.

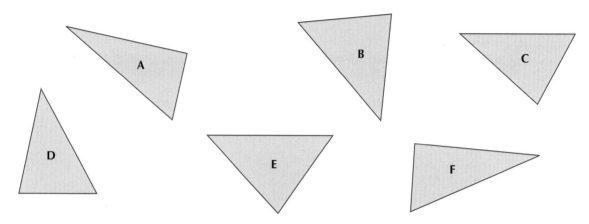

2 Which shapes are congruent? Write your answer like this, e.g. A = D = F.

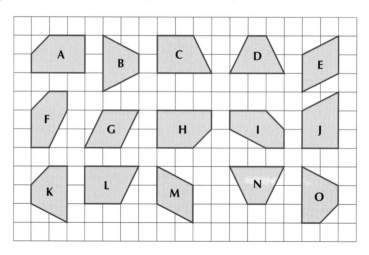

3 **a** Use triangular dotted paper. Draw 15 shapes by joining some of the dots as shown in the diagram. Label your shapes from A to N.

b Write down the shapes that are congruent.

1 **a** Describe the single transformation
that maps
  i A onto F
  ii D onto A
  iii C onto A
  iv E onto F
  v D onto B.
  b Describe the combination of two
transformations that maps
  i A onto D
  ii B onto C
  iii E onto G.

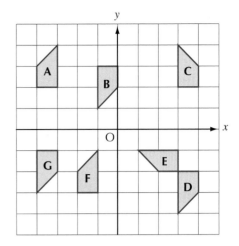

2 **a** Copy this diagram onto square paper.

  b Reflect triangle A in the dotted mirror line and
label the image B.

  c Reflect triangle B in the x-axis and label the
image C.
  d What single transformation maps shape A onto
shape C?

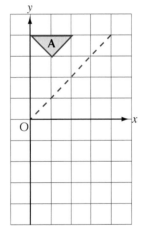

3 **a** Reflect shape A in the y-axis and
label the image B.
  b What combination of two
transformations maps shape A
onto shape B?

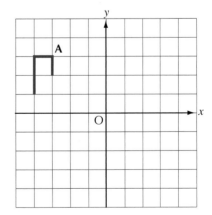

4 **a** Which single transformation maps a shape onto itself?
  b Describe a combination of two transformations that map a shape
onto itself.

1 Trace each shape with its centre of enlargement O. Enlarge the shape by the given scale factor.

Scale factor –3   Scale factor –2

2 Copy each diagram and enlarge the shape about the point C using the given scale factor.

a

Scale factor –2

b

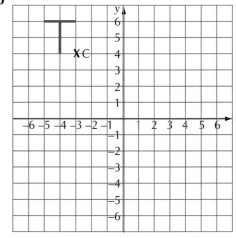

Scale factor –4

3 Shape A′B′C′D′ is the enlargement of shape ABCD using a scale factor of –2. Find the points A, B, C and D using rays and draw the shape ABCD.

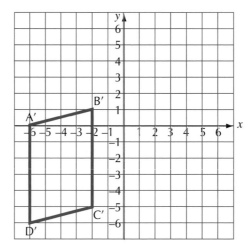

Practice

9D Planes of symmetry

1 Write down the number of planes of symmetry that each shape has.

a

3 cm

3 cm

b

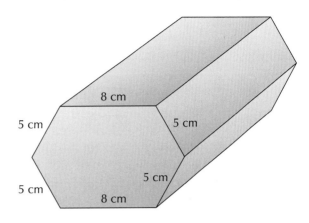

8 cm

5 cm

5 cm

5 cm

5 cm

8 cm

2 Sketch a solid with exactly one plane of symmetry. Use dotted lines to show the plane of symmetry.

3 Copy each shape using an isometric grid. Draw a plane of symmetry using dotted lines or shading. Make a copy of the shape for every plane of symmetry.

a

b

c

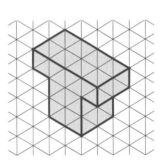

Practice

9E Shape and ratio

Express all ratio answers in their simplest form.

1 Express each of these ratios in its simplest form.

    a 90 cm : 20 cm   **b** 32 mm : 72 mm   **c** 150 cm : 2 m

    d 1.8 cm : 40 mm   **e** 0.65 km : 800 m

2

a Find the ratio of the base of rectangle A to rectangle B.
b Find the ratio of the area of rectangle A to rectangle B.
c What fraction is area A of area B?
d Find the ratio of the area of rectangle B to rectangle C.
e Which is greater: area A as a fraction of area B or area B as a fraction of area C?

3 This diagram shows the design of a new flag.

a Calculate the ratio of the white area to the blue area.
   Use ratios to answer these questions.
b 60 m² of white cloth is used to make some flags.
   How much blue cloth was needed?
c The total area of some flags is 200 m².
   i   How much white cloth do they contain?
   ii How much blue cloth do they contain?

4 This diagram shows the plan of a garden.

a Find the ratio of the perimeter of the fence to the perimeter of the pool.
b Calculate the area of the pool.
c Calculate the area of the lawn.
d Find the ratio of the lawn area to the pool area.

10A Solving equations

1 Solve these equations.

    a $3a + 7 = 13$ **b** $2n - 3 = 11$ **c** $5v - 20 = 30$

    d $6x + 5 = 29$ **e** $10c - 17 = 73$ **f** $19 = 2y + 13$

2 Solve these equations.

    a $8 + 3t = 23$ **b** $6 + 5m = 16$ **c** $9 + 4d = 29$

    d $13 + 8s = 101$ **e** $43 + 2z = 51$ **f** $63 = 7 + 7i$

3 Solve these equations. The answers are decimals or fractions.

    a $4q + 1 = 15$ **b** $5h - 3 = 3$ **c** $10y + 21 = 69$

    d $3f - 2 = 5$ **e** $8e + 5 = 19$ **f** $5 = 5w - 9$

4 Solve these equations. Expand the brackets first.

    a $2(n + 1) = 12$ **b** $5(p - 2) = 25$ **c** $4(g + 3) = 44$

    d $3(2r + 1) = 15$ **e** $2(3b - 7) = 4$ **f** $70 = 5(4i + 2)$

5 Solve the equations in Question 4 again. This time, remove the brackets by dividing both sides by a number.

6 Solve these equations. Use any method you like.

    a $4r - 20 = 8$ **b** $9 = 5x + 2$ **c** $4(y + 4) = 24$

    d $3 + 5a = 48$ **e** $3(5h - 8) = 36$ **f** $7 + 4u = 25$

7 Helmut's homework and solutions are shown below. Explain what is wrong with each solution. Find the correct answer, where necessary.

Questions	
a $9x - 2 = 25$	a $9x - 2 = 25 + 2 = 3$
b $3 + 4y = 19$	b $3 + 4y = 19$
	$4y = 19 + 3 = 22$
	$y = 5.5$
c $2(2x - 3) = 14$	c $2(2x - 3) = 14$
	$4x - 3 = 14$
	$4x = 17$
	$x = 4.25$

10B Equations involving negative numbers

Solve these equations.

1   **a** $3x + 11 = 2$ **b** $2y + 15 = 3$ **c** $4a + 6 = 2$ **d** $15 = 5C + 40$

2   **a** $12 + 3x = 6$ **b** $6 + 5b = 31$ **c** $22 + 6m = 4$ **d** $36 = 100 + 16q$

3   **a** $4d - 19 = -3$ **b** $2x + 7 = -3$ **c** $3z - 14 = -32$ **d** $-22 = 5t - 12$

4   **a** $-4i = 28$ **b** $-3H = 6$ **c** $-8k = -16$ **d** $30 = -6x$

5   **a** $6 - 4x = 18$ **b** $1 - 7u = 15$ **c** $3 - 3d = -12$ **d** $16 = 8 - 2m$

6   Expand the brackets first.

     a $4(s + 2) = 4$ **b** $3(m - 5) = -6$
     c $2(3n + 9) = 6$ **d** $-10 = 5(2y - 12)$

7   **a** $-5x = 10$ **b** $8 - 5x = -12$ **c** $12 + 5f = -3$
     d $2(x + 3) = -10$ **e** $-1 = 3w - 7$ **f** $4(2d - 1) = -36$

Practice

10C Equations with unknown terms on both sides

Solve these equations.

1   **a** $5y = 9 + 2y$ **b** $10x = 20 + 6x$
     c $8u = 3u + 25$ **d** $7p = 3p + 32$

2   **a** $20 - 3x = x$ **b** $12 - 2c = 2c$
     c $4d = 30 - d$ **d** $5p = 14 - 2p$

3   **a** $6g + 5 = 2g + 13$ **b** $9i + 7 = 5i + 19$
     c $10h - 3 = 3h + 18$ **d** $8t - 15 = 6t + 3$

4   **a** $35 + 2k = 9k$ **b** $3x + 8 = 5x$
     c $2x + 23 = 7x + 3$ **d** $r + 16 = 5r - 10$

5   These equations involve negative numbers.

     a $8y = 6y - 10$ **b** $6k - 6 = 9k$ **c** $40 + 7j = 2j$
     d $5d + 9 = 3d + 3$ **e** $-4r = 3r + 21$ **f** $7n - 3 = 3n - 15$

6   Expand the brackets first.

     a $3(x + 2) = 2x + 8$ **b** $3(2g + 3) = 4g + 17$
     c $5(s - 2) = 3(s + 4)$ **d** $8w - 12 = 3(3w - 1)$

Practice

10D Substituting into expressions

1   Write down the value of each expression for each value of x.

     a $3 + 4x$ when
        i $x = 2$ **ii** $x = 7$ **iii** $x = -3$
     b $9p - 2$ when
        i $p = -4$ **ii** $p = 0$ **iii** $p = 8$
     c d^2 when
        i $d = 7$ **ii** $d = -6$ **iii** $d = -1$
     d $2s^2$ when
        i $s = 3$ **ii** $s = 10$ **iii** $s = -2$
     e $m^2 - 5$ when
        i $m = 4$ **ii** $m = 1$ **iii** $m = -4$
     f $5(3n - 2)$ when
        i $n = 2$ **ii** $n = 0$ **iii** $n = -5$

2 If $p = 3$ and $q = 5$, find the value of each of these expressions.

    a $2q - p$ **b** $q + 3p$ **c** $p^2 + q^2$

    d $4(3p - q)$ **e** $2q - (4p - q)$

3 If $r = -2$ and $s = 3$, find the value of each of these expressions.

    a $2r + s$ **b** $r - 2s$ **c** $3(2r + 3s)$

    d $r - (2s + 1)$ **e** $10s + 2(r - s)$

4 If $m = 2$ and $n = -4$, find the value of each of these expressions.

    a $n^2 - m^2$ **b** $5m^2$ **c** mn^2

    d $5mn - m^2$ **e** $m^2 - (2m - n)$

5 If $x = 3$, $y = 5$ and $z = -2$ find the value of each of these expressions.

    a xyz **b** $xz + y$ **c** $2x - 3y - 4z$

    d $(x - z)(x + y)$ **e** $xz + y(2x - z)$

Practice

10E Substituting into formulae

1 The ideal weight, W kg, of a man of height h cm is given by this formula:

$W = 0.75h - 67.5$.

Calculate the ideal weight of a man of height

    a   160 cm   **b**   186 cm   **c**   1.7 m

2 Given that $C = F + 4d$, find the value of C when

    a $F = 12, d = 6$ **b** $F = 200, d = 65$ **c** $F = 18, d = -3$

3 The cost of a sheet of glass is given by the formula $C = 3bh$ where C is the cost (£), b the breadth and h the height in metres.

Calculate the cost of these sheets of glass:
    a   breadth 2 m, height 4 m
    b   breadth 3 m, height 1.5 m
    c   breadth 0.3 m, height 0.8 m.

4 Given that

$$W = \frac{2m + 2n + p}{2}$$

calculate the value of W when

    a $m = 4, n = 2, p = 6$
    b $m = -3, n = 2, p = 5$
    c $m = 6, n = -1, p = -4$

5 The approximate area of a circle of radius r is given by the formula $A = 3r^2$ where A is the area and r is the radius.

Find the area of a circle of radius
    a   5 cm   **b**   2.5 cm   **c**   0.9 cm

1 Write an expression for each of these, using the letters suggested.

    a The sum of the numbers d and 3.
    b The number u reduced by 5.
    c The product of the numbers w, 7 and s.
    d One third of the number m.
    e The number of toes on f feet.

2 How many metres are there in x centimetres?

3 Michael is H cm tall now.

    a He was 5 cm shorter a year ago. How tall was he then?
    b In 3 years' time, he will be x cm taller. How tall will he be then?
    His taller sister Briony has a height of S cm.
    c How much taller is Briony?
    d What is the average height of Michael and Briony?

4 **a** A Chocolate Wheel costs c pence and a Frother costs f pence.
       What is the total cost of
       i a Chocolate Wheel and a Frother?
       ii 5 Frothers?
       iii 3 Chocolate Wheels and 2 Frothers?
    b How much change from a £2 coin would you receive for each of the purchases in **a**?
    c A packet of Fruit Spots costs 5p more than Frothers.
       i What is the total cost of 3 packets of Fruit Spots?
       ii How many packets of Fruit Spots can be bought for £2?
       iii How much more do 2 Chocolate Wheels cost than a packet of Fruit Spots?
       iv There are 10 Fruit Spots in a packet. How much does each Fruit Spot cost?
    d 4 Frothers cost 40p more than a packet of Fruit Spots. Find the cost of a Frother.
    Hint: Write an equation and solve it.

5 Kevin spent T pence on text messages one week. Marit spent 30p more than Kevin. Akemi spent twice as much as Kevin.

    a How much did they spend altogether?
    b If they spent 270p altogether, how much did Kevin spend?
    Hint: Write an equation and solve it.

6 Mr Walker's daughter is x years old. Five years ago, Mr Walker was twice as old as his daughter and their ages added up to 57.

    a What were their ages five years ago?
    b What was the total of their ages five years ago?
    c Find the age of Mr Walker's daughter.
    Hint: Write an equation and solve it.

Practice
11A Statistical surveys

Conduct a statistical investigation to test one of the hypotheses below.
Your investigation must include a questionnaire.
*   Write down three or four good questions for your questionnaire
*   Make a data recording sheet.
*   Collect information from at least 30 people.

1 Girls eat more fruit than boys.

2 Pupils prefer more English lessons or more Maths lessons.

3 Year 7 pupils watch less football than Year 8 pupils.

4 People visit the cinema once a year, on average.

5 People think crime has increased in their area.

Practice
11B Stem-and-leaf diagrams

1 The average speeds of 35 racing cars are shown in this stem-and-leaf diagram.

11	0	9	9	9								
12	1	2	2	3	4	4	5	6	6	6	8	9
13	0	4	4	5	5	6	6	7	8	8	8	8	9
14	0	3	3	6	8	9						

Key:
14|3 means
143 km/h

   a What is the mode?
   b Find the median.
   c Calculate the range.
   d The qualifying speed for the next race is 136 km/h.
      How many cars qualified?

2 The ages of 25 children are shown in this stem-and-leaf diagram.

11	9 9 9 10 11 11
12	0 0 1 2 2 3 4 5 7 10 10 10
13	0 3 3 4 5

Key:
12|4 means
12 years and 4 months.

Note: months are rounded down to the nearest month.
a How many children are 12 years old?
b How many children are younger than $12\frac{1}{2}$?
c Calculate the mode, median and range.

3 These are the weights of 27 letters (in grams).

48	29	62	48	96	45	30	59	16
88	63	10	74	64	38	90	25	8
44	92	67	78	33	50	23	60	18

a Make a stem-and-leaf diagram for the data. Remember to show the key.
b State the mode.
c Calculate the range.
d Find the median.
e Letters weighing 60 g or more are charged 41p for first class delivery.
  How many letters need this postage?

Practice

11C Interpreting graphs and diagrams

1 Draw pie charts to represent the data.

a The numbers of birds spotted on a field trip.

Bird	Crow	Thrush	Starling	Magpie	Other
Frequency	19	12	8	2	19

b The sizes of dresses sold in a shop during one week

Size	8	10	12	14	16	18
Frequency	3	7	10	12	6	2

2 150 children went on one of four
school summer holidays.
How many children chose these
holidays?

a Camping
b France
c Pony trekking
d DisneyWorld

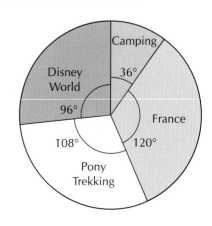

3 The grouped bar chart shows the average number of text messages people make using their mobile phones during a month.

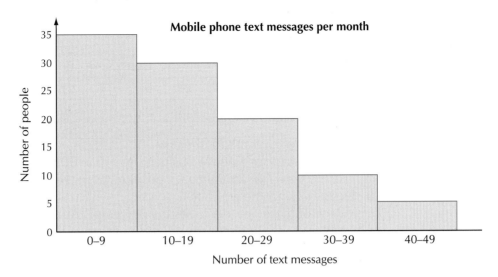

Mobile phone text messages per month

y-axis: Number of people

*x-axis: Number of text messages (0–9, 10–19, 20–29, 30–39, 40–49)*

a *Mobile Weekly* magazine claim that 50% of people make more than 25 text messages per month. Could this be true?

b Is it possible that more people make no text messages than those who make 30 text messages or more?

c Is it true to say that the most frequent number of text messages made is between 0 and 9, inclusive?

d Write down two more observations based on the diagram.

4 Chin Lin asked 20 people which instrument they prefer to listen to.
She drew this pie chart to show the results.

Favourite instrument

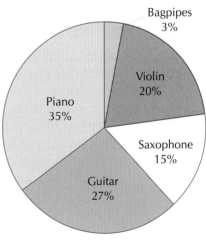

a Roughly half the people chose two of the instruments. Which two?

b Sean says that at least 5 people prefer to listen to the saxophone. Is he correct?

c The violin is more popular than the bagpipes and saxophone combined. Is this true?

d Just over twice the number of people chose the piano compared to another instrument. Which instrument?

e Stringed instruments are twice as popular compared to wind instruments. Is this true? **Note:** stringed instruments include the piano.

f Write down two more comparisons based on the pie chart.

g Chin Lin made two mistakes in her diagram. What are they?

11D Scatter graphs

1. This table shows the class positions of pupils in their Science and Mathematics classes.

Pupil	Jo	Ken	Lim	Tony	Dee	Sam	Pat	Les	Kay	Val	Rod
Science	24	3	13	21	5	15	22	7	12	27	14
Maths	20	5	10	14	9	15	26	1	16	24	11

   a Draw a scatter graph for the data.
      Use the x-axis for Science position, from 0 to 30.
      Use the y-axis for Mathematics position, from 0 to 30.
   b Describe what the graph tells you.
   c Which of these best describes the degree of correlation:
      positive correlation, negative correlation, no correlation?

2. This table shows the heights and history test scores of 20 children.

Height (cm)	130	110	160	120	120	140	160	150	110	130	140	120	170	150	140	160	110	150	140	140
Score	13	19	12	14	7	20	14	10	9	3	17	20	20	15	8	6	13	20	6	12

   a Draw a scatter graph for the data.
      Use the x-axis for height, from 100 cm to 170 cm.
      Use the y-axis for history test score, from 0 to 20.
   b Describe what the graph tells you.
   c Describe the degree of correlation.

11E Analysing data

For each question below:
*   Write a hypothesis.
*   Decide how best to collect the data (questionnaire, experiment, secondary sources, e.g. books, newspapers).
*   Make a data recording sheet. Collect the data.
*   Organise your data into tables, etc.
*   Draw diagrams to illustrate your data.
*   Make any necessary calculations, e.g. mean, range.
*   Write a conclusion.

1. How many times can you catch a ball with your weaker hand before dropping it?

2. Do we eat more vegetables now, compared to 10 years ago?

3. How often do people eat from a barbecue?

4. Are the leaves at the bottom of a plant bigger than the leaves in the middle?

5. How long does it take the average person to travel to work?

12A Fractions

1 Copy and complete these.

    a $\dfrac{9}{4} = \dfrac{\square}{12}$
          b $\dfrac{20}{3} = \dfrac{180}{\square}$

    c $\dfrac{11}{2} = \dfrac{99}{\square}$
          d $\dfrac{32}{7} = \dfrac{\square}{35}$

    e $\dfrac{100}{28} = \dfrac{\square}{7}$
          f $\dfrac{144}{18} = \dfrac{24}{\square}$

2 **a** How many fifths are in $3\frac{4}{5}$?

    b How many thirds are in $7\frac{1}{3}$?

    c How many twelfths are in $4\frac{7}{12}$?

    d How many sevenths are in 32?

3 Write each of these as a mixed number in its simplest form.

    a $\dfrac{13}{5}$
          b $\dfrac{32}{3}$
          c $\dfrac{28}{9}$

    d $\dfrac{40}{6}$
          e $\dfrac{60}{8}$
          f $\dfrac{84}{18}$

    g $\dfrac{133}{21}$
          h thirteen thirds
          i eighteen eighths

4 Write each of these as a fraction.

    a The fraction of a litre given by

        i 320 cl
        ii 645 cl
        iii 272 cl
        iv 9375 ml

    b The fraction of a foot (ft) given by

        i 20 in
        ii 51 in
        iii 100 in
        iv 114 in

5 Convert each of these fractions to an improper (top-heavy) fraction.

    a $1\frac{4}{5}$
        b $2\frac{1}{3}$
        c $4\frac{3}{10}$
        d $33\frac{1}{3}$
        e $5\frac{2}{7}$

12B Adding and subtracting fractions

If necessary, convert your answers to mixed numbers and cancel down.

1 Use an eighths fraction line to calculate these.

    a $\frac{7}{8} + \frac{3}{4}$
    b $1\frac{5}{8} + 2\frac{7}{8}$
    c $1\frac{1}{4} - \frac{3}{8}$
    d $3\frac{1}{2} - 1\frac{5}{8}$
    e $2\frac{1}{4} + 1\frac{3}{8} - 2\frac{5}{8}$

2 Calculate these.

a $\frac{2}{7} + \frac{3}{7}$ b $\frac{11}{12} - \frac{7}{12}$ c $\frac{4}{5} + \frac{3}{5} + \frac{4}{5}$ d $\frac{5}{8} + \frac{7}{8} - \frac{3}{8}$

3 Convert the fractions to equivalent fractions with a common denominator. Then calculate the answer.

a $\frac{1}{5} + \frac{1}{2}$ b $\frac{1}{10} + \frac{2}{5}$ c $\frac{5}{6} + \frac{4}{9}$

d $\frac{3}{8} + \frac{5}{6} + \frac{1}{4}$ e $\frac{3}{4} - \frac{1}{3}$ f $\frac{11}{12} - \frac{3}{4}$

g $\frac{7}{9} - \frac{1}{3}$ h $\frac{9}{10} - \frac{1}{2} - \frac{1}{5}$

4 Convert the mixed numbers to improper (top-heavy) fractions. Then calculate the answer.

a $2\frac{3}{5} + 1\frac{1}{2}$ b $1\frac{5}{6} + 3\frac{1}{4}$ c $4\frac{2}{3} - 1\frac{3}{4}$ d $3\frac{3}{8} - 1\frac{1}{6}$

5 Of Jan's emails, $\frac{3}{5}$ is junk mail and $\frac{1}{10}$ is from friends. The rest is work related.

a What fraction is work related?
b Jan received 120 emails during the week. How many were *not* junk mail?

6 A poster is printed using red, blue and yellow inks. Of the ink used, $\frac{2}{9}$ is red and $\frac{1}{6}$ is blue.

a What fraction of the ink used is *not* yellow?
b 36 ml of ink is used to print the poster. Calculate the amount of each ink used.

7 Sharon bought a bag of flour weighing $3\frac{3}{4}$ kg. She used $\frac{7}{10}$ kg for a cake and $1\frac{3}{5}$ kg for some bread.

a How much flour did she use altogether?
b How much flour did she have left over?

Practice

12C BODMAS

Do not use a calculator. Show all of your working.

1 Write down the operation that you would do first in each calculation. Then calculate the answer.

a $12 - 3 \times 2$ b $2 \times (9 - 5)$ c $10 \times 2 \div 5 + 3$
d $30 - 20 + 10$ e $12 + 8 - 3^2$ f $4 \times (2 + 5)^2$

2 Calculate these. Show each step of your calculation.

a $3^2 + 5 \times 2$ b $10 - (1 + 2)^2$ c $3 \times 12 \div 3^2$

d $32 \div (3^2 - 1)$ e $\frac{60 + 12}{2 \times 3}$ f $\frac{60}{(6 + 3^2)}$

g $1.5 + 3 \times (2.4 - 0.8) - 2.1$

3 Copy each calculation. Insert brackets to make the answer true.

    a $11 - 7 - 1 + 4 = 1$ **b** $1 + 4 + 3^2 = 50$

    c $24 \div 2 \times 3 = 4$ **d** $6 + 9 \div 12 \div 4 = 5$

    e $12 - 3^2 - 7 \times 4 = 4$

4 Calculate these. Work out the inside brackets first.

    a $120 - [70 - (90 - 55)]$ **b** $[(2 + 7)^2 - 12] \div 3$

    c $(2 + 6) \times [36 \div (9 - 5)]$ **d** $12^2 - [5^2 - 2 \times (32 - 27)]$

Practice

12D Multiplying decimals

Do not use a calculator.

1 Calculate these.

    a 200×0.9 **b** 0.8×400 **c** 500×0.09

    d 2000×0.7 **e** 0.006×600 **f** 70×0.04

    g $90\,000 \times 0.004$ **h** 3000×0.002 **i** 0.0004×400

2 Calculate these.

    a $300 \times 0.4 \times 0.8$ **b** $0.006 \times 7000 \times 0.2$

    c $0.04 \times 0.07 \times 300$ **d** $30\,000 \times 0.002 \times 0.04$

3 Calculate these.

    a 0.6×0.7 **b** 0.9×0.9 **c** 0.05×0.7 **d** 0.8×0.03

    e 0.4^2 **f** 0.04×0.09 **g** 0.003×0.6 **h** 0.008×0.002

4   **a** 0.24×7.5 **b** 0.46×0.32 **c** 12.1×0.18 **d** 23.4×11.7

5 A seed weighs 0.04 g. How much does a box of 600 seeds weigh if the box alone weighs 17 g?

6 Sound travels about 0.3 km in 1 second. How far does sound travel in

    a 200 seconds   **b** 10 minutes   **c** 0.02 seconds?

    Work in kilometres.

7 Ham costs £8.31 per kg. How much does 0.18 kg cost? Round your answer to the nearest 1p.

Practice

12E Dividing decimals

Do not use a calculator.

1 Calculate these.

    a $0.6 \div 0.03$ **b** $0.08 \div 0.5$ **c** $0.36 \div 0.04$ **d** $0.9 \div 0.02$

    e $0.04 \div 0.001$ **f** $0.15 \div 0.002$ **g** $0.07 \div 0.05$ **h** $0.8 \div 0.002$

2 Calculate these.

   a $9 \div 0.3$ **b** $40 \div 0.8$ **c** $60 \div 0.015$ **d** $48 \div 0.12$
   e $500 \div 0.025$ **f** $900 \div 0.003$ **g** $5000 \div 0.02$ **h** $120 \div 0.24$

3 Calculate these.

   a $2.8 \div 20$ **b** $32 \div 800$ **c** $1.2 \div 300$
   d $0.16 \div 400$ **e** $0.54 \div 90$ **f** $0.008 \div 400$

4 Calculate these.

   a $35.2 \div 1.1$ **b** $11.7 \div 2.6$ **c** $3.12 \div 4.8$ **d** $13.23 \div 2.7$

5 0.008 g of platinum costs £0.16. Calculate the cost of 1 g. Work in pounds.

6 A website gives 3.6p to charity on every sale it makes. In one month, the website gives £86.40 to charity. How many sales did it make?

7 **a** 3000 bacteria have a mass of 0.000 003 g. What is the mass of one bacterium (bacteria is the plural of bacterium)?
   b 10 000 000 000 000 atoms have the same mass as one bacterium. What is the mass of an atom?

CHAPTER **13** Algebra 5

Practice

13A Expand and simplify

For Questions 1–3, simplify these expressions.

1 **a** $4p + 7p$ **b** $9u - 3u$ **c** $7d - d$
   d $3i + 5i + 8i$ **e** $4n + 5n - 5n$ **f** $10h - 7h - h$
   g $2f - 7f$ **h** $-6y - 3y$ **i** $2d - 5d - 5d$

2 **a** $7s + 2s + 4t$ **b** $9i - 4i + 2j$ **c** $4a + 3b + 2b$
   d $5d + 4y + 3d$ **e** $6r + 3h - 4r$ **f** $5b + 3d - 7d$
   g $5u + 2a + 3u + 4a$ **h** $4d + 5y - 2y + 3d$
   i $10k + 4p - 7k - 2p$ **j** $6t - 3g + 2t - 4g$

3 Expand these expressions.

   a $4(x + 8)$ **b** $7(3d - 5)$ **c** $2(4f + 2e)$
   d $d(3 - u)$ **e** $m(2r + c)$ **f** $j(3h - 2g)$

For Questions 4–5, expand and simplify these expressions.

4 **a** $2x + 3(x + 5)$ **b** $4d + 2(5d + 6)$ **c** $9i - 4(i + 2)$
   d $7u - 3(2u - 3)$ **e** $6k + 2e + 3(2k + e)$ **f** $4a + 7b - 2(5a - 2b)$

5　**a**　$3(4i + 2) + 4(i + 2)$

　　b　$3(2s + 3) + 2(s - 4)$

　　c　$2(3i - 5) + 3(4i - 1)$

　　d　$4(2s + 3) - 3(s + 2)$

　　e　$5(2f + 2) - 3(3f - 3)$

　　f　$4(3 + 2g) - 3(2 - 4g)$

6　Solve these equations.

　　a　$2(d + 1) + 3(d + 2) = 23$

　　b　$3(2s + 5) + 4(s - 3) = 43$

　　c　$3(3w + 2) - 2(2w - 1) = 28$

　　d　$2(2k + 3) - 3(k + 1) = 1$

Practice

13B Solving equations by trial and improvement

1　Solve the equation $x^2 + x = 80$, giving your answer correct to
1 decimal place. Copy and complete this table.

x	$x^2 + x$	Comment
8	$8^2 + 8 = 72$	too small
9		
8.5		
8.4		
8.45		
8.46		

2　Solve these equations, giving your answer correct to 1 decimal place.
Make a table for each equation.

　　a　$x^2 + x = 40$　　**b**　$x^2 - x = 66$　　**c**　$x^3 + x = 7$　　**d**　$x^3 - x = 20$

Practice

13C Constructing equations

1　**a**　A book and writing pad cost £8 altogether. The book costs £x.
　　　Write an expression for the cost of the writing pad.

　　b　Maria is twice the age of Janine. Janine is j years old.
　　　Write an expression for the age of Maria.

　　c　The difference between the heights of two trees is 4 m. The taller tree is
　　　T metres high. Write an expression for the height of the shorter tree.

2　Solve each of these problems by creating an equation and then solving it.

　　a　Tyres cost £x each. 4 tyres cost £112.
　　　Find the cost of one tyre.

　　b　Jamie is y years old and Paul is 9 years old. Their ages total 16 years.
　　　How old is Jamie?

　　c　The difference between two numbers is 5. The smaller number is n and
　　　the larger number is 12.
　　　What is the smaller number?

　　d　A plum weighs p grams. A lemon weighs 12 g more than the plum.
　　　i　Write an expression for the total weight of the lemon and plum.
　　　ii　If the total weight is 44 g, find the weight of the plum.

e A soap opera lasts 3 times as long as a cartoon. The cartoon lasts m minutes. The soap opera and the cartoon last 32 minutes altogether.
  i Write an expression for the total length of the programmes.
  ii The soap opera and the cartoon last 32 minutes altogether. How long does the cartoon last?

f The sum of three consecutive numbers is 78. The smallest number is n. Find the value of n.

g I am x years old. Three times my age 4 years ago is 27. How old am I?

h A bakery sold 15 boxes of cakes. Large boxes contain 4 cakes and small boxes contain 3 cakes. 51 cakes were sold altogether. How many large boxes were sold?
Hint: Let the number of large boxes be x.

Practice

13D Problems with graphs

1 Find the gradient of each of these lines.

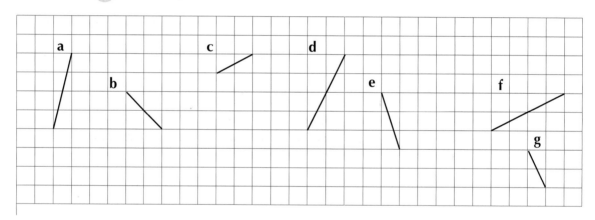

2 Find the gradient of the straight line that joins each pair of coordinates. You may need to plot the points using squared paper.

  a (1, 4) and (3, 10)   **b** (2, 10) and (4, 2)   **c** (0, 3) and (6, 6)
  d (−3, 2) and (0, 8)   **e** (−1, 6) and (1, −6)

3 Find the gradient and y-axis for each of these equations.

  a $y = 3x + 5$ **b** $y = -2x + 3$ **c** $y = 0.5x - 3$ **d** $y = 3x$

4 Write the equation of each line in the form $y = mx + c$, given this information.

  a $m = 5, c = 2$ **b** gradient is 6, y-intercept is −3
  c gradient is −3, y-intercept is 9   **d** gradient is 1.2, y-intercept is 0

5 Find the gradient, y-intercept and equation for each graph below.

   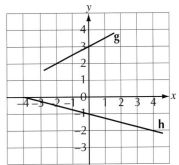

6 Draw the graph of each equation using the gradient and y-intercept. Do *not* calculate any coordinates.

a $y = 2x + 3$ **b** $y = x - 4$ **c** $y = -3x + 4$ **d** $y = -2x - 1$

Practice **13E Real-life graphs**

1 Sketch a graph to illustrate each of these situations. Estimate any necessary measurements.

a The height of a person from birth to age 30 years
b The temperature in summer from midnight to midnight
c The height of water in a WC cistern from before it is flushed to afterwards

2 This diagram shows the cost of car hire for two companies.

a Estimate the cost of hiring a car from each company and travelling
   i 60 miles   **ii** 100 miles   **iii** 240 miles
b Describe the way each company charges for car hire.
c When is Cheap Hire cheaper than Square Deal Cars?

3 Match each description to its graph.

    a The temperature of the desert over a 24-hour period
    b The temperature of a kitchen over a 24-hour period
    c The temperature of pond during a month of winter
    d The temperature of a cup of tea as it cools down

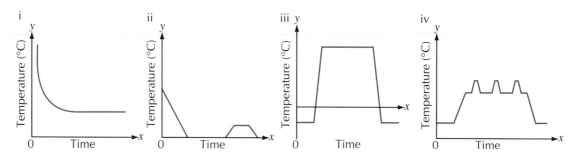

4 George tried several diets to lose weight. This table shows his weight loss over a one-year period. He weighed 105 kg at the beginning of the year.

Diet	Weight loss/gain
Hay diet	Lost 10 kg in 2 months
Calorie counter	Stayed same weight for 3 months
Vegetarian	Gained 3 kg in 2 months
Usual diet	Gained 12 kg in 1 month
Atkins diet	Lost 28 kg in 4 months

Draw a graph showing how George's weight changed over time.
Start the vertical weight axis at 80 kg and use a scale of 1 cm to 2 kg.

Practice

13F Change of subject

1 Rewrite each of these formulae as indicated.

    a $T = D + H$; express H in terms of T and D.
    b $m = \frac{d}{e}$; express d in terms of m and e.
    c $PV = kT$; express T in terms of P, V and k.
    d $R = r - s$: express s in terms of R and r.

2 Rewrite each of these formulae as indicated.

    a $A = \pi r^2$; make π the subject of the formula.
    b $y = mx + c$; make c the subject of the formula.
    c $A + B = 2C$; make C the subject of the formula.
    d $y = mx + c$; make m the subject of the formula.
    e $T = 4(m - n)$; make m the subject of the formula.

3 The perimeter of a shape is given by the formula $P = 4a + 5b$.

    a   Find the value of P when $a = 4$ cm and $b = 7$ cm.
    b   Make b the subject of the formula.
    c   Calculate the value of b when $a = 6$ cm and $P = 38$ cm.

4 The speed of a car is u mph. It accelerates for t seconds to a speed of v mph. Its final speed v mph is given by the formula $v = u + 4t$.

    a   Calculate the final speed of the car if it accelerates from 20 mph for 5 seconds.
    b   Make t the subject of the formula.
    c   How long does it take the car to accelerate from 10 mph to 80 mph?

5 The formula $A = \dfrac{a + b}{2}$ calculates the average A of two numbers a and b.

    a   Find A when $a = 5$ and $b = 9$.
    b   Make a the subject of the formula.
    c   The average, A, of two numbers a and 18 is 12. Use your formula to find a.

CHAPTER 14   Solving Problems

Practice

14A Number and measures

1 Two pens and a pencil have a total length of 49 cm. Four pens and a pencil have a total length of 77 cm.
What is the total length of seven pens and a pencil?

2 Copy and complete this puzzle so that each large triangle adds up to 50.

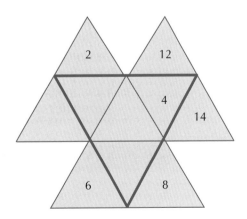

3 Harry's car can travel 320 miles on a full tank of petrol. He drives 124 miles from Harwich to Dover and then 330 km to the Hook of Holland. Does he need to stop for petrol?

4 a   Find three consecutive even numbers that add up to 114.
    b   Find two consecutive even numbers with a product of 1088.

5 A bag of potatoes in the UK weighs 15 lb. A bag of potatoes in France weighs 7 kg. Which is heavier?

6 Two 12-hour electric clocks start at 12 noon. Clock A loses 5 minutes every hour. Clock B keeps perfect time.

   a What will be the time showing on clock A when clock B next reaches 12 o'clock?
   b How long will it take before both clocks show 12 o'clock again?

14B Using algebra, graphs and diagrams to solve problems

1 A pond is 240 cm deep. The depth of the pond decreases 2 cm every day.

   a How long before the pond is half its original depth?
   b Write a formula to show the depth D cm of the pond in n days.

2 I think of a number, treble it and then subtract 24. The answer is 27. What was the number I first thought of?

3 Five times the number I am thinking of is 16 more than treble the number. What is the number I am thinking of?

4 A fruit bowl weighs 500 g and holds oranges that weigh 200 g each.

   a Write a formula to show the total weight W of n oranges.
   b Draw a graph to show the total weight of the fruit bowl and oranges.
      Use the x axis for Number of Pieces of Fruit, numbered from 0 to 7.
      Use the y axis for Weight, numbered from 0 to 2000 g.
      Another fruit bowl weighs 800 g and holds apples that weigh 100 g each.
   c Draw another graph *using the same axes* to show the total weight of a bowl of apples.
   d Use your graphs to find when a bowl of oranges weighs the same as a bowl of apples.

5 **a** Fold an A4 sheet of paper into three equal parts. Fold the folded sheet in half. Open the sheet and count the rectangles.
   b Repeat part **a** but, this time, fold the folded sheet in half twice.
   c Write down a formula for the number N of rectangles made by folding the folded sheet in half n times.
   d How many rectangles would be made by folding the A4 sheet 5 times?
   e How many times would you have to fold the sheet to make 200 rectangles or more?

14C Logic and proof

1 Copy and complete these number problems.

a
```
  □ 5 □
+ 1 □ 7
───────
  4 4 6
```

b
```
    3 □
×   □ 4
───────
  8 8 8
```

c $7\,□^2 = □\,9\,□\,9$

d $(10 + □)(□ + 8) = 182$

2 **a** Give an example to show that the product of three odd numbers is odd.
   b Prove that the product of three odd numbers is odd.
   Hint: Remember the product of two odd numbers.

3 **a** Give an example to show that the product of two odd numbers with two even numbers is even.
   b Prove that the product of the product of four numbers – two odd and two even – is even.

4 **a** List the factors of 21.
   b Prove that all of the factors of an odd number are odd.

5 It takes 8 people 12 hours to dig a hole. How long would it take

   a 4 people   **b** 2 people   **c** 6 people?

6 6 glasses hold 120 cl altogether. 8 mugs hold 144 cl altogether.
   Which holds the most, a mug or a glass?

7 Which of these numbers must be odd? Explain your answer using algebra.

   a $6n$ **b** $4n - 1$ **c** $2n + 5$ **d** $n + 3$

   Note: n is any positive integer.

8 Use algebra to prove that subtracting an even number from 20 leaves an even number.

9 Use algebra to prove that multiplying an odd number by 3 gives another odd number.

10 Use algebra to prove that squaring an even number gives an even number.

Practice

14D Proportion

1 Two of the carriages on a train are first class. The other six carriages are second class.

   a What proportion of carriages are first class?
   b What is the ratio of first class to second class carriages?
   A train with 12 carriages has the same proportion of first class carriages.
   c How many first class carriages does it have?

2 The ratio of nitrogen to oxygen in the air is approximately 4 : 1.
   A cupboard contains 600 litres of air.

   a How much nitrogen does it contain?
   b How much oxygen does it contain?

3 8 light bulbs cost £7.20. How much does a box of 20 light bulbs cost?

4 There are three females for every four males in a social club with 91 members. How many females are there?

5 2 gallons is approximately 9 litres.

    a How many gallons are equivalent to 63 litres?
    b How many litres are equivalent to 7.5 gallons?

6 8 grams of silver are used to make 15 cm of chain.

    a How much silver does 21 cm of chain contain?
    b How long is a chain that contains 25 grams of silver?

7 A photo of area 108 cm^2 is enlarged to have an area of 180 cm^2. What is the ratio of the two areas?

8 12 kg of a new metal alloy was made using this formula:

Tin	400 g
Copper	3 kg
Lead	1800 g
Iron	6.8 kg

Calculate the formula to make 21 kg of the metal alloy.

Practice

14E Ratio

1 Simplify these ratios.

    a 12 : 9   **b** 16 : 30
    c 18 kg : 42 kg   **d** £4 : 75p
    e 8 weeks : 12 days   **f** 45 cm to 3 m
    g 5 kg : 1.75 kg

2 **a** Express these ratios in the form $n : 1$.
       i 18 : 3   **ii** 16 : 10   **iii** 9 : 15   **iv** 400 : 125
    b Express the same ratios in the form $1 : n$.

3 **a** Divide 40 cm in the ratio 7 : 1.
    b Divide 600 mm in the ratio 11 : 9.
    c Divide 5000 people in the ratio 3 : 5.
    d Divide £76 in the ratio 2 : 7 : 10.

4 Donna eats three times more hot meals than cold meals. She eats 96 meals in July. How many of them were hot?

5 The ratio of children in Year 8 who own a mobile phone to those who do not is 3 : 2. There are 210 children in Year 8.
How many children do *not* own a mobile phone?

6 The land area to sea area of the surface of the Earth is in the ratio 3 : 7.
The total surface area of the Earth is 500 000 000 km^2.
What is the area of land?

7 Marcia receives 12 items of junk mail for every 5 letters. Rajid receives
9 pieces of junk mail for every 4 letters.

    a Write the ratio of junk mail to letters for each person in the form $n : 1$.
    b Who receives the greater proportion of junk mail?

CHAPTER 15 Shape, Space and Measures 4

Practice

15A Plans and elevations

1 Draw each of these 3D shapes on an isometric grid.

a

b

c

2 For each of these 3D shapes, draw a **i** plan **ii** front elevation **iii** side
elevation.

a

b

3 The plan, front and side elevations of a 3D shape are shown below. Draw the solid on an isometric grid.

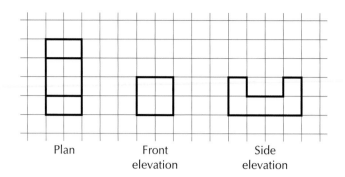

Plan   Front
elevation

Side
elevation

4 The diagram shows two views of the same solid.

Draw enough plan and elevation diagrams for someone to follow to make the shape out of plastic cubes.

Practice

15B Scale drawings

1 These objects have been drawn using the scales shown. Find the true lengths of the objects.

a   1 cm to 10 cm

b   2 cm to 1 m

c   1 cm to 0.7 m

d   2 cm to 3 m

2

Scale: 1 cm to 120 m

The diagram shows a scale drawing of an aircraft hanger.

a   Calculate the real length of the hanger.
b   Calculate the real width of the hanger.
c   Calculate the area of the hanger.

3 Copy and complete this table.

	Scale	Scaled length	Actual length
a	1 cm to 2 m		24 m
b	1 cm to 5 km	9.2 cm	
c		12 cm	42 miles
d	5 cm to 8 m	30 cm	

4 This diagram shows a scale drawing of a supermarket.

Make a table showing the dimensions and area of each section of the supermarket.

1 Copy this grid and plot the points.

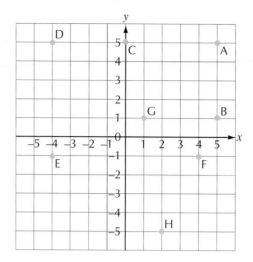

a List the coordinates of the points.
b Join these pairs of points using straight lines.
    i AB   **ii** AD   **iii** DE   **iv** EF
    v AG   **vi** EH   **vii** BE
c Find the mid-point of each line in **b**.
d List the coordinates of the mid-points.

2 Copy this grid and plot the points.

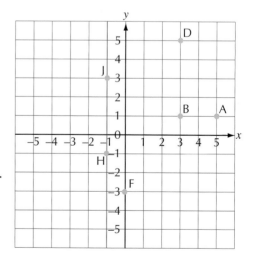

a B is the mid-point of line AC.
    Find the coordinates of point C.
b B is the mid-point of line DE.
    Find the coordinates of point E.
c F is the mid-point of line EG.
    Find the coordinates of point G.
d J is the mid-point of line DK.
    Find the coordinates of point K.
e The origin is the mid-point of KL.
    Find the coordinates of point L.

3 Find the mid-points of these line segments. Use any method you know
(diagram or calculation).

    a A(1, 3) joined to B(5, 7)   **b** C(0, 4) joined to D(5, 8)
    c E(–4, 0) joined to F(0, 6)   **d** G(–6, –2) joined to H(2, –4)

1 Write each of these map scales as a map ratio, i.e. 1 : number.

   a 1 cm to 3 km   **b** 1 cm to 100 m   **c** 2 cm to 100 km

2 This map shows an area of England and Wales. Find the shortest (straight line) distance between these pairs of places. Give your answers to the nearest 5 km.

Scale:
|⎯⎯⎯|
1 cm : 30 km

   a Liverpool and York   **b** Coventry and Bangor
   c Worcester and Leeds   **d** Lincoln and Stoke-on-Trent

3 The distance between Knutsford and Littleborough is 42 km.
   How far apart would these towns be on the above map?

4 Barry made a journey using these motorways.
   Nottingham to Leicester on the M1
   Leicester to Coventry on the M69
   Coventry to Stoke-on-Trent on the M6

   Use a piece of string on the above map to estimate the total length of his journey, to the nearest 10 km.

5 The ratio of a map is 1 : 200 000.

   a Two places are 15 cm apart on the map. What is their actual distance apart?
   b Two places are 71 km apart. How far apart are they on the map?

1 Sketch loci for these. Describe each locus.

    a A moving garden swing.

    b A moving ski lift chair.

2 This diagram shows three wooden balls in a game of bowls. Trace the diagram.

    a A fourth ball, D, moves equidistant from balls A and B. Sketch its locus.

    b A fifth ball collides with the balls. Ball C moves so that it is equidistant from the edge of the bowling green. Sketch its locus.

3

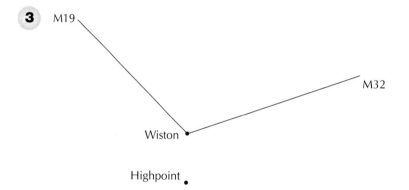

Stan drives his car from Highpoint, heading eastwards, and keeps the same distance from Wiston. When Stan is equidistant from the motorways, he drives away from Wiston, keeping equidistant from the motorways. Trace the diagram and sketch the locus of Stan's car.

4 Mark a point on the circumference of a 2p coin. Move the coin along the edge of a ruler. Draw the locus of the marked point.

5 The wheel continuously runs along this channel, staying in contact with the edge Y.

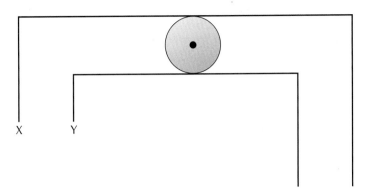

X   Y

    a Trace the diagram.
    b Draw the locus of the centre of the wheel.

Practice

15F Bearings

1 Use your protractor to find the bearing of B from A.

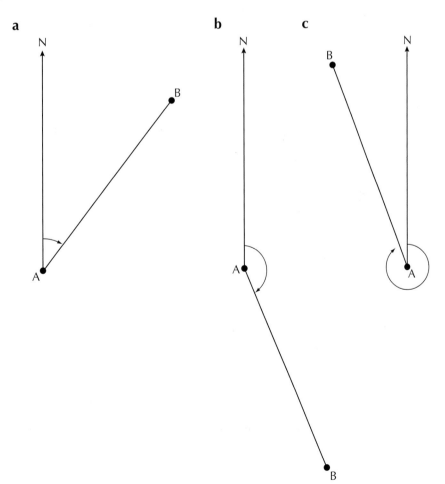

a

b   **c**

2 Find the bearing of P from Q.

3

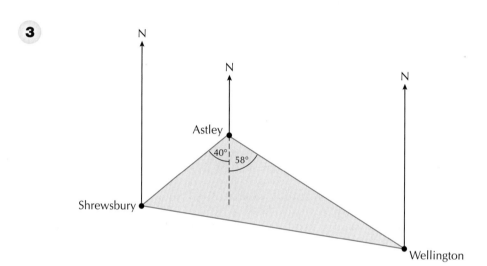

Calculate the bearing of

a Wellington from Astley   **b** Astley from Wellington
c Astley from Shrewsbury   **d** Shrewsbury from Astley.

Use your protractor to find the bearing of

e Wellington from Shrewsbury   **f** Shrewsbury from Wellington.

4 Sketch these bearings. Label your diagrams.

    a A skier is on a bearing of 072° from the ski lodge.
    b Clerkhill is 12 miles from Moffat on a bearing of 115°.

CHAPTER 16

Handling Data 3

16A Collecting data for frequency tables

1. This table shows the lengths (*L* metres) of 30 python snakes.

Length of snake (*L* metres)	Frequency
$3.5 \leqslant L < 4$	2
$4 \leqslant L < 4.5$	4
$4.5 \leqslant L < 5$	7
$5 \leqslant L < 5.5$	9
$5.5 \leqslant L < 6$	5
$6 \leqslant L < 6.5$	3

   a One of the snakes is 4.5 m long. Which class contains this length?
   b How many snakes are shorter than 5 metres?
   c How many snakes have a length of 5.5 metres or more?
   d How many snakes are between 4 and 6 metres long?
   e Why is your answer to **d** an approximation?

2. The volumes (*V* cl) of liquid contained in 20 coconuts are shown below.

12.2	11.1	10.5	12.8	12.0	10.1	11.8	12.3	10.7	12.7
10.0	11.6	12.1	10.5	10.8	12.6	10.7	11.4	12.8	11.3

   Copy and complete this table.

Volume of liquid (*V* cl)	Tally	Number of coconuts
$10 \leqslant V < 10.5$		
$10.5 \leqslant V < 11$		
$11 \leqslant V < 11.5$		
$11.5 \leqslant V < 12$		
$12 \leqslant V < 12.5$		
$12.5 \leqslant V < 13$		

3. The durations (*t* minutes) of 30 telephone calls are shown below. Times have been rounded up to the nearest minute.

4	12	8	1	19	7	7	28	14	54
9	2	20	16	2	43	5	18	1	5
5	14	9	10	3	30	11	6	17	2

   Construct a grouped frequency data for the data.

4 Describe in detail how you would collect data to investigate each of these.

    a The bounce of a ball dropped from different heights

    b Most people find that alternative medicine doesn't work.

    c It is cheaper to use public transport than to travel by car.

Practice

16B Assumed mean and working with statistics

1 **a** Find the mean of 256, 251, 259, 250, 255, 255, 253, 249.
Use 250 as assumed mean.

    b Find the mean of 72.7, 72, 72.9, 71.7, 72.8, 72.3, 72.6, 72.2, 72.6, 72.2. Use 72 as assumed mean.

    c Find the mean of 58 284, 58 280, 58 287, 58 278, 58 289.
Use 58 280 as assumed mean.

2 Write down two numbers with a range of 4 and a mean of 7.

3 Write down three numbers with a mode of 10 and a mean of 9.

4 The mean of four numbers is 5, the mode 1 and the range is 11.
What are the four numbers?

5 The mode of a set of numbers is 5, their range is 10 and their mean is 20.
Each of the numbers is increased by 10.

    a How are the averages affected?

    b What is the new range?

6 The weekly wages of four employees are £320, £290, £420 and £370.

    a Calculate the mean and range for the wages.

    b The employer hires a fifth worker. She wants the mean wage to be £340.
What should she pay the fifth worker?

    c All workers received a pay rise of £30 per week. How will this affect the mean and range (do not recalculate them)?

    d The next year, the workers receive a 10% pay rise. How do you think the mean and range will be affected?

Practice

16C Drawing frequency diagrams

1 Draw a bar chart for each frequency table.

    a Amounts of beer served in 500 ml glasses.

Amount of beer (V ml)	Number of glasses
$485 \leqslant V < 490$	3
$490 \leqslant V < 495$	7
$495 \leqslant V < 500$	13
$500 \leqslant V < 505$	18
$505 \leqslant V < 510$	11

Price of beach ball (£ P)	Number of shops
£2.80 $< P \leqslant$ £3	27
£3 $< P \leqslant$ £3.20	51
£3.20 $< P \leqslant$ £3.40	30
£3.40 $< P \leqslant$ £3.60	23
£3.60 $< P \leqslant$ £3.80	13
£3.80 $< P \leqslant$ £4	9

2 This table shows the average height of a sweet corn bush after being sprayed with different amounts of a new additive.

Amount of additive (A ml)	Height of plant (h m)
0	1.40
10	1.40
20	1.45
30	1.55
40	1.70
50	1.70
60	1.60
70	1.50
80	1.40
90	1.30
100	1.30
110	1.30

a Plot a graph. Use these scales.
x-axis (Amount of additive): 1 cm to 10 ml
y-axis (Height of plant): 2 cm to 0.10 m
b Estimate the level of additive that would give plants of height 1.65 m.
c Estimate the height of a plant sprayed with 75 ml of additive.
d Which level of additive would you advise the farmer to use? Explain your answer.
e At which levels did the additive not improve growth?

Practice

16D Comparing data

1 QuickDrive and Ground Works are two companies that lay drives.
The numbers of days taken to complete 9 drives each are shown below.

QuickDrive   2, 5, 3, 3, 6, 2, 1, 8, 3

Ground Works   3, 2, 3, 1, 4, 3, 2, 2, 1

a Calculate the mode, mean and range for each company.
b Comment on the differences between the averages.
c Comment on the difference between the ranges.

2 This table shows the weights of fish (grams) that three anglers caught in a competition.

Jerry	Aditya	Marion
230	230	100
100	400	130
380	280	430
720	320	200
450	250	70
		180
		200
		90

a   Calculate the mean and range for each of the anglers.
b   Who was the most consistent? Explain your answer.
c   Who performed the best overall? Explain your answer.
d   Which angler would you choose to enter a competition that offered prizes for the heaviest fish caught? Explain your answer.

3 This table shows the mean and range for the average weekly rainfall (mm) in two holiday resorts.

	Larmidor	Tutu Island
Mean	6.5	5
Range	33	62

Explain the advantages of each island's climate using the mean and range.

Practice

16E Comparing sets of data

1 These pie charts show how two companies first contacted new customers.

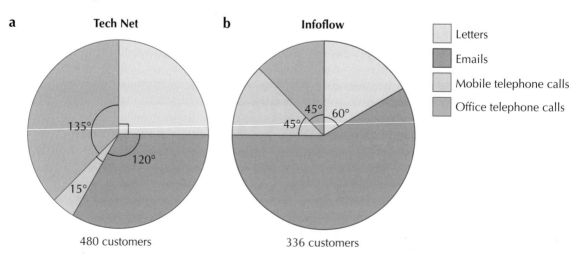

a   **Tech Net**
b   **Infoflow**

135° 120° 15°

45° 45° 60°

☐ Letters
☐ Emails
☐ Mobile telephone calls
☐ Office telephone calls

480 customers   336 customers

Explain your answers to these questions.

  a Which company sent the most emails?

  b Which company made the most telephone calls?

  c Make two more comparisons between the companies.

2 This bar chart shows the lengths of holidays sold by two shops.

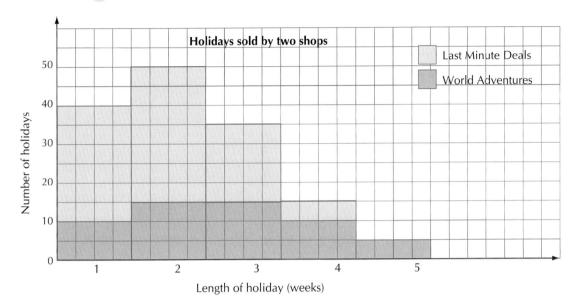

Write a report comparing the sales of the two shops.

3 This graph shows the number of salmon caught at a fishing lodge during 1990 and 1995.

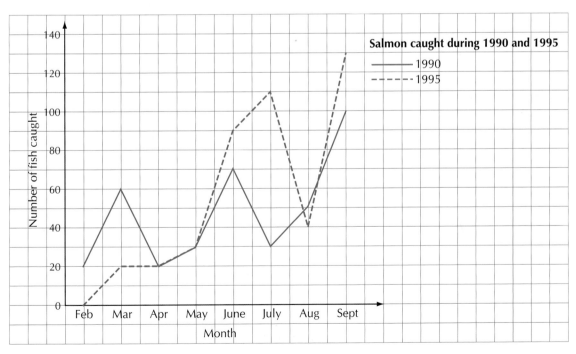

  a Make a table of the data.

  b Write a report comparing the catches during 1990 and 1995.

1 Copy this set of raffle ticket numbers. Use three rows as shown.

1	2	3	4	5	6	7	8	9	10
11	12	13	14	15	16	17	18	19	20
21	22	23	24	25	26	27	28	29	30

a What is the theoretical probability of someone choosing a number between 11 and 20 (inclusively)?

b Design and carry out an investigation to test this hypothesis:
People are most likely to choose a number from the middle row.

2 a Roll a dice until you get an odd number.
What is the theoretical probability that the next roll will be odd too?

b Design and carry out an experiment to test this hypothesis.
An odd number is more likely to be followed by an even number than by an odd number.